ALSO BY MOOREA SEAL

the 52 Lists project

52 Lists for Happiness

Make Yourself at Home

DESIGN YOUR SPACE to DISCOVER YOUR TRUE SELF

MOOREA SEAL

Photographs by **MARISSA MAHARAJ**

Illustrations by **JULIA MANCHIK**

SASQUATCH BOOKS
SEATTLE

TO MY MOM AND DAD, who were the first in my life to teach me what home truly means. No matter where we lived or how great or small our pocketbook was at the time, my parents created spaces that fully reflected our depth of love for one another and provided for our needs even when it was a challenge. They cultivated beauty, life, and vibrancy in our homes growing up that felt so different from anyone else I knew and 100 percent just like us as a family. They taught me that it's not only okay to stand out and to feel different, but important to celebrate differences; enjoy the exploration of self-discovery and self-knowledge; create, cultivate, design, style, and play kinesthetically in making spaces and the self feel true, fresh, and alive; and love others' uniqueness as we should, and can, love our own unique perspectives.

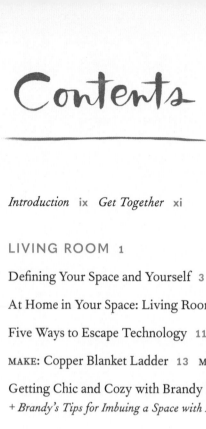

Contents

Introduction ix   *Get Together* xi

LIVING ROOM 1

Defining Your Space and Yourself 3

At Home in Your Space: Living Room 9

Five Ways to Escape Technology 11

MAKE: Copper Blanket Ladder 13   MAKE: Essential Oil Diffuser 15

Getting Chic and Cozy with Brandy Brown 19
+ Brandy's Tips for Imbuing a Space with Elegance and Whimsy 25

KITCHEN 27

Finding Peace in Process 29

At Home in Your Space: Kitchen 35

Five Kitchen Decorating Tips to Inspire Self-Investment 37

MAKE: Herb Drying Rack 38   MAKE: Floral Ice Cubes 41

Looking on the Bright Side with Diana La Counte 43
+ Diana's Tips for Adding Joy and Humor to Your Home 49

DINING ROOM 51

Celebrating Friendship and Family 53

At Home in Your Space: Dining Room 59

Ten Tips for Hosting an Affordable, Beautiful, and
Memorable Dinner Party 60

MAKE: Gold-Patterned Glassware 63   MAKE: Macramé Wall Hanging 65

Collected Treasures with Brooke Eide 69
+ Brooke's Tips for Thrifting on Craigslist 75

OFFICE 77

Nurturing Professional Growth 79

At Home in Your Space: Office 85

Ten Motivational Quotes 87

MAKE: Ikea Desk Hack 89 MAKE: Marbled Leather Mouse Pad 93

Multipurpose Work Spaces with Kim Kogane 95
+ *Kim's Tips for Being a Leader in Your Life* 103

BEDROOM 105

Creating a Private Sanctuary 107

At Home in Your Space: Bedroom 113

Deep Sleep Playlist 115

MAKE: North Star Mirror 117 MAKE: Copper Pipe Necklace Display 121

Vintage Vibes with Erin Perez Hagstrom 125
+ *Erin's Tips for Buying Pieces to Last a Lifetime* 133

NATURE 135

Bringing the Outside In 137

At Home in Your Space: Nature 143

Five Easy-Care Indoor Plants 144

Ten Natural Elements You Don't Have to Water 147

MAKE: Moon Phase Wall Hanging 148 MAKE: Nature Gallery Wall 153

Getting Green with Laura Gummerman 157
+ *Laura's Tips for Decorating with Plants* 165

Acknowledgments 167 *At Home with Color* 168

At Home with Style 178 *At Home with Vintage Eras* 180

Resources 185 *Index* 191

Introduction

I HAVE MOVED ALMOST EVERY SINGLE year for the last ten years of my life, and one year I even moved twice! As a result, I've come to understand that when I don't feel settled in my space, I don't feel settled in myself. Can you relate? Our houses become *homes* once we spend time investing in them, adding our unique touches to our environment and creating memories within our four walls. The same goes for how we invest in ourselves. When we don't take time to get to know ourselves and invest in our own inner worlds, we can often lose track of who we are, what brings us joy, and what makes us feel unique and valuable. For me, taking time to cultivate a comfortable and beautiful space in my home directly reflects how I feel about myself. When I am tired and stressed, my home gets messy and cluttered. When I am feeling centered and at peace, it shows in the clean and tidy state of my home. And when I've just moved into a new house or have been living there for a while, not sure how to decorate or where to begin, I feel deeply uncomfortable—both within myself and in the place I hope to call home. It's not a great feeling, but it can be remedied by simply following your intuition!

Decorating your home isn't just about making a room look pretty; it's about creating an environment that is true to you and that inspires you to invest in yourself in the way that you have invested in your space. Within these pages, I'll share with you not only my advice for transforming each room of your house into a dwelling that reflects who you are, what you need, and what you love, but also tips on how to develop a deeper love of self and understanding of your personal story as you transform the spaces around you. I've been through a lot in my thirty-one years. And I hope that by sharing my personal stories about my life and my home, and those of the other amazing women in this book, I will encourage you to trust more deeply in your instincts and follow your journey toward self-discovery.

No matter where you are in your life, no matter how much money you have or how big or small the space is that you call home, you can create something that truly reflects who *you* are in a beautiful way. It takes time; it takes thoughtfulness and contemplation of what brings you joy, comfort, celebration, peace, and inspiration. But as we move through each room together, you'll have a chance to discover what stories you want to tell with your décor. They're waiting inside of you, ready to be unlocked and shared within your favorite spaces. So come on in, and make yourself at home.

Xo Moorea Seal

Get Together

YOU'RE NOT ALONE IN YOUR JOURNEY of investing in your home while investing in yourself. There is a whole community of people who are thoughtfully cultivating a comfortable, creative home and an inspired life!

Use the hashtag **#MakeYourselfAtHomeBook** on social media to find other people who are also working their way through this book alongside you! Discover continued inspiration from our community and connect with fellow readers by sharing snaps of your book, your completed DIYs, and your one-of-a-kind homes on social media.

You can find me just about everywhere at @mooreaseal and MooreaSeal.com. I'm so excited to see how *Make Yourself at Home* inspires your life and encourages you to thrive within your home and within yourself.

Living Room

Defining Your Space and Yourself

I LIKE TO THINK OF THE LIVING ROOM as the anchor to a house (or apartment, or trailer, or tree house—wherever it is that you call home). It's typically the first space where guests get a peek into your personal world. In a living room, you get to define yourself and what you love, and present that to those who enter your home. If you live alone, you're lucky to get to share your full, unique perspective! And if you live with someone else, be it a partner or a roommate, your living room represents your collective inner world.

In my own living room, I can see the bold statements and subtle nuances that make it truly feel like me and the union I have with my husband, somewhere that we can unwind over a glass of wine and a movie, laugh over a board game, or stay up late reflecting on the places we've been and what lies ahead for our family. He trusts my styling intuition, and I always consider what he may or may not like in the décor I choose. Lucky for me, he is kind, considerate, and adaptable, and our style is naturally very similar. One of my sisters also lives with us too! She's definitely patient with me and my strong opinions on décor and design. But between the three of us, we have found a common design theme in what we love through a textured and rustic-bohemian, but tidy, aesthetic. This space is an expression of our eclectic personalities and tastes, and it shows what defines each of us in our passions and our quiet moments as individuals just as much as it reflects us as a community of people within a home. And in styling our communal living room, our goal is to make it feel welcoming to old friends and new, in the hopes that friendships will grow more deeply as we get to know one another in this shared space.

Our living room is a visual map of who we are. We care about depth of character, so we chose rich colors, tones, and textures. We also care about investing in family, friends, comfort, and warmth, and we have pieces that evoke these sentiments, ranging from a coffee table that's a hand-me-down from an elderly woman I was close to growing up, to a leather butterfly chair from my friends at the globally inspired, handmade home-décor company The Citizenry that I got when they first launched their brand online. Every time I look at it, I am reminded of all the women in business whom I admire and support. My Moroccan-style ottoman was a treasure I found at a flea market here in Seattle called Fremont Sunday Market, where I used to sell my own jewelry when I was starting out as a small business. It reminds me of where I've been, the hard work needed to make your dreams happen, and the beauty you can shape along your creative journey.

In many ways, defining and decorating your living room is similar to the process of discovering your authentic self. Fortunately, forging your identity is not something that many of us have to do all in one go (and decorating your living room doesn't need to be either!). We get our whole lifetimes to practice, experiment, and continue to redefine who we are and what is important to us. As kids, we had so many opportunities to play around with expressing ourselves, like rearranging our bedroom, adding our favorite stickers to our binder, or tasting foods we ended up loving or hating. It was a lot easier back then to make bold moves in defining who we were and who we wanted to be. For me, as a child, defining who I was amid wild transitions that were outside of my control was of the utmost importance.

At nine years old, I decided that I wanted to change my name. It wasn't a momentary phase of defiance toward my parents; it culminated from a lot of powerful, difficult experiences that left me feeling like I needed to do something dramatic to regain a feeling of control. When I was two, we had moved to a rural village of four hundred people in England—and I consider it my first home and the place that shaped my inner world. I was determined and strong-willed but still a very shy and gentle person with a vivid imagination. The village and schools I grew up in nurtured and supported my quiet and creative spirit. But, sadly, we couldn't afford to stay beyond my eighth birthday. My dad wasn't paid enough to support our family of four. My family had to move back to the United States in order to live a better life, and it came as a massive shock to me.

In the summer of 1994, we left the rolling farmlands of rural England for the mountains and pine trees of a historical mining town in the Sierra Nevadas of California called Nevada City. The visuals of the landscape felt foreign to me, as did the culture. I went from a private prep school in England that felt like Hogwarts to a California public school where fifth graders were smoking weed in the bathrooms. Most of the boys and girls in my class were abrasive and aggressive, and the schoolwork was so confusing for me even though everyone

else seemed to be catching on quickly. I also didn't understand American culture, what clothes were cool, what TV shows and music everyone loved, what personalities were accepted or teased. I spoke English and had American parents just like most of my classmates, but culturally, and in a new physical environment, I was completely lost and afraid.

By the end of my first year in the United States, I had also lost multiple friends my age to completely random, unrelated, and tragic deaths. That trauma was overwhelming on top of the move. It was just too much for an eight-year-old to handle. So what did I do? I changed my name. I was desperately trying to express my authentic self amid so much confusion and chaos. Thankfully, I was fortunate to have a dad who challenged me to take ownership of my life, even when it was scary or difficult. When he told me my youngest sister was going to have Moorea as a middle name, after the Tahitian island, I said, "That sounds like me! I want to change my name to Moorea." He told me that if I could get everyone at my school to call me Moorea by the end of the quarter, then I could change it. And when my report card came back with "Moorea Seal" as my name instead of Ashley, my dad stuck to his word and chose a different middle name for my youngest sister.

When I changed my name, I was claiming my identity. Out with the old Ashley and in with the new Moorea. My parents say that, along with my name change, my personality shifted in subtle but powerful ways too. My confidence rose, my belief in what I could achieve skyrocketed, and self-respect and understanding returned. With one grand decision at a young age came the realization that, even when life felt out of control, I always had the opportunity to make a positive choice. It was a monumental challenge for a timid girl—convincing my teachers, family, and friends that I wanted to be called by a different name. But I did it. I believed that my self-expression was valid and worth pursuing. And what do you know? That name has gone on to become my brand name too!

Just as I sought to define who I was within myself, and then present it to the world, I have the same resolve to imbue my living spaces with self-expression. And the balance of vibrancy and peace in my living room reflects how I see myself inside—a blend of peaceful and nurturing versus determined and headstrong. I juxtapose more "masculine" elements like deeper paint palettes; dark wood; rich leathers; and even animal skulls with lighter, more "feminine" pieces such as soft sheepskin; warm and welcoming tones of red, cream, and beige; and touches of shine with copper and brass accents. My living room conveys both my sensitive, artistic, and creative soul and my assertive and driven sense of self, the part of me that has built my business up to where it is today. Just like how I have designed my women's retail store here in Seattle, my living room is both comfortable for us and our guests yet visually stimulating and eclectic.

The more I get to know myself as the years come and go, the more my living room grows with me, reflecting the memories I hold dear and the people, places, and experiences that have made an impression on my life. The best example of that is probably the vintage artwork hanging above my couch—not only a nod to my love of everything from the seventies with its retro colors and quirky fonts, but something that unifies my husband, my sister, and me in this space, since it's a map of our hometown. While it may not sound like an ideal living arrangement, particularly for a newly married woman, living with a sibling and a spouse at the same time, we all get along and it's proof that your life needn't be "perfect" in order for you to build a beautiful and harmonious living space. This piece of art represents our love and respect for one another in our shared

home, and memories of the place where we all grew up. (I went to high school with my husband but didn't date him until much later.) It also reflects my own coming to terms with—and appreciation for—my move from England to the United States. I now cannot be more grateful for where I grew up, which ultimately led me to the man I love most. When people visit our home, it feels so special to me that so many objects in our home are visual representations of what is most important to us. Our friends and new acquaintances glean so much about who we are not only from what we say but how our home tells a story. And our living room is the first place where that story of who we are as individuals and as a family begins.

At Home in Your Space

LIVING ROOM

What do you want *your* living room to say about who you are, be it to close friends and family or acquaintances you're just getting to know? As you contemplate that question, take a moment to look around your living room. Is it missing that *special* touch of who you define yourself to be? You may just find that perfect something packed away in the dark depths of your basement, in a DIY project you've been meaning to finish, or in a letter from someone you love waiting to be framed. Or maybe it's a vintage treasure hidden away at a flea market that you've yet to find. Let your mind wander . . . What does your living room say about you?

Consider your own space as you ponder these questions. Feel free to use the Notes section in the back of the book for journaling or sketching out ideas.

- What does "living" mean to you?

- What were your favorite memorable moments in your living room growing up?

- What activities do you want to encourage yourself to do in this space? Is there something you feel like you want to do but never have enough time for?

- What statement does your living room currently make about you and your values?

- What mood/vibe/feeling do you want your living room to have?

- What colors reflect that mood?

- What decorative items do you already have that connect to that mood?

- What sorts of scents/candles do you like to have in this space?

It's so easy to fall into the trap of just using your living room to watch TV or mindlessly browse the internet on your iPad. And while there's certainly a time for that, there's a reason it's called a living room—and you probably want your life to be more than just technology! Since tech devices are usually front and center in these spaces and can be all too tempting, here are some ways to set up your living room to give yourself more incentive to spend less time in the virtual world and more time in the real one.

FIVE WAYS TO ESCAPE TECHNOLOGY

1 Keep a list of fun activities you want to do outside of your house by your front door, on either a chalkboard or a framed piece of paper. It will remind you that getting out of the house is just as important as taking time to rest at home.

2 Keep a cute pair of sneakers by your door to encourage yourself to go on more walks. I've got to admit I'm not the sportiest person and I rarely have the inspiration to buy athletic shoes or clothes, let alone wear them. But once I found some cute, seventies-inspired tennis shoes that kind of matched the colors of my living room, I was happy to have them on display and more eager to find a reason to wear them.

3 Incorporate one or more of your favorite activities into your décor. I keep lots of paintbrushes, colored pencils, paints, and stickers in clear jars and on brass trays by my desk at home, and I occasionally like to bring them out into my living room to remind myself to play and have fun artistically. When I'm bored, seeing the things that bring me joy creatively inspires me to try something new. If you are a music lover, invest in a cool record player for your living room. Not only do records sound great, but they make for rad art and décor in your space as well. Or try keeping a stack of games in your living room that you can easily grab to play after dinner with your partner, roommates, or friends.

4 Place your to-read stack or a few of your all-time favorite books near where you keep your TV, computer, iPad (or other techie toys) in your living room to inspire you to pick up a book once in a while instead of turning on the TV or browsing the internet to find entertainment.

5 Hide your TV—use a hutch with doors or hang a tapestry from the top of your TV that you can flip up or down. If it isn't the focal point of the room, you'll be less likely to automatically turn it on. Out of sight, out of mind!

Make: COPPER BLANKET LADDER

This simple copper ladder isn't just lovely; it's functional as well. Prop it up against a wall to hold colorful patterned blankets, towels, or, in my case, family heirloom rugs that my dog has chewed in spots but that I can't bear to let go.

STEPS

1. Peel off any stickers from the copper. Use the Goo Gone to clean off any sticky residue.

2. Take four of the 1½-foot-long poles and connect them vertically with three pressure tees. Repeat for the second side of the ladder.

3. Attach the three remaining poles to the two sides of the ladder by inserting them into the open ends of the pressure tees. This adds the three ladder steps.

4. Attach the end caps to the tops and bottoms of the ladder.

5. If joints aren't nice and tight, reinforce by lightly adding superglue to the inside edges of the caps and tees.

TIP: Clean any tarnish on copper with a salt and lemon juice mixture. Scrub it over the area and let it sit for 15 seconds or for as long as needed to remove tarnish. Then rub with a damp cloth. (You can do this any time if tarnishing occurs.)

MATERIALS AND TOOLS

11 (1½-foot-long) pieces ¾-inch-thick copper pipe (have your pipe cut at a local hardware store)

Goo Gone

6 (¾-inch) copper pressure tees

4 (¾-inch) copper end caps

Superglue (optional)

For information on where to buy materials and tools, see Resources (page 185).

Make: ESSENTIAL OIL DIFFUSER

You've probably seen these in home goods stores, and they're an easy way to add a dreamy scent to your home without having to worry about leaving something burning. However, they can be quite expensive, which is why I like to make my own. Plus, by doing it yourself, you can create your own signature scent—which your guests will remember whenever they walk into your house.

STEPS

1. Wash the diffuser jar with soap and water.

2. Test mixing essential oil scents by dropping one to five drops of each oil together in one spot on a paper towel. Experiment and see if certain oils are stronger smelling than others and decide which ones you like best, be it several together or one on its own.

3. Add the almond or fractionated coconut oil to the diffuser jar. (You will be mixing the oils together in step 5. If the opening of your jar is too small, mix the oils in a bowl first and then use a funnel to add them to the jar.)

4. Add the essential oils on top. The goal is to have 70 percent base oil and 30 percent essential oils.

5. Mix the oils together with one of the diffuser sticks.

6. Add five to eight diffuser sticks to the jar, depending on how strong you want the scent to be in your room. Over time, the oils will travel up the sticks and warm your space with delicious scents.

7. Flip the sticks anytime the tops feel dry, or to just give your room an extra boost of heady aroma!

> **TIP:** Fractionated coconut oil is composed of capric and caprylic acids, which help extend the shelf life and give it rancidity-resistant properties. It remains in liquid form.

MATERIALS AND TOOLS

4-ounce diffuser jar or small glass jar with small opening (opening should be smaller than ¾ inch in diameter so as not to allow moisture to escape from the jar too rapidly)

Dish soap and water

1.6 ounce bottles of essential oils (a variety of your choice)

Paper towels

3.5 ounces sweet almond oil or fractionated coconut oil, as a base oil (I purchased a 16-ounce bottle of fractionated coconut oil to make multiple diffusers)

Bowl (optional)

Funnel (optional)

5–8 diffuser sticks

For information on where to buy materials and tools, see Resources (page 185).

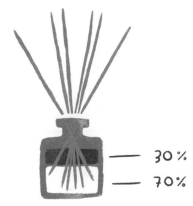

30 %

70 %

. . . *continued*

MY FAVORITE ESSENTIAL OIL COMBINATIONS

Vetiver + Amber + Rose

I love the combination of vetiver, amber, and rose. It's actually almost the same as my store's signature scented candle that we created with P. F. Candle Co.: lightly perfumy and warm, feminine but woodsy. Rose is said to help in dealing with panic attacks, handling stress and grief, warming the spirit, and inspiring comfort. Vetiver, with its rich and earthy notes, helps with insomnia, anxiety, and insecurity. And amber not only cleanses your environment but is said to aid in pain relief. Amber can be very powerful, so go easy on it when using it in combination with other notes.

Bergamot + Patchouli

This combination is a beautiful balance of that classic earl gray (a floral and just slightly citrusy scent) balanced with an earthier tone found in patchouli. Bergamot helps to combat anger, anxiety, depression, stress, fatigue, fear, insecurity, and loneliness and helps boost self-confidence while inspiring peace and happiness. Patchouli also taps into similar emotional spaces, encouraging peace and calming feelings. Maybe that's one of the many reasons why it was such a popular scent during the hippie movement in the sixties and seventies!

Lavender + Eucalyptus

Lavender is a classic scent that so many people love, refreshing and comforting all at once. Many use lavender to help with sleep and to combat headaches, and paired with the soothing scent of eucalyptus, it makes a great combo to put beside your bed as you fall asleep. Eucalyptus is said to help with memory and concentration, which also makes this great for drifting off to sleep, helping you process your day through your nightly dreaming.

Lemon + Lime

Both lemon and lime are major mood boosters, igniting energy, positivity, and clarity, and they always leave me feeling so refreshed. This is my favorite combo to keep in my bathroom, always making a room feel fresh, clean, and bright.

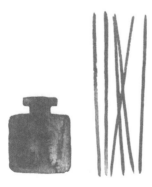

GETTING CHIC AND COZY WITH
Brandy Brown

BRANDY BROWN

Creative director, graphic designer, and blogger

LIVES IN: Seattle, Washington

FROM: Tacoma, Washington

SIGNATURE STYLE: French provincial meets modern contemporary

WHAT SHE LOVES: organization, without a doubt—function and good form encourage clarity and positive energy; statement art, gilded knickknacks (the older the better!), fresh flowers, and natural elements

WHERE SHE FINDS INSPIRATION: life is a series of inspirations, which can strike at any moment—she finds beauty in the details and strives to garner these occasions; the opportunities to collaborate and create are endless

Brandy Brown is one of the most positive people I know. Even if she's talking about something profound or difficult, she always finds a way to remain upbeat and smiling. I think that quality is what makes her the world's greatest host and entertainer, and the joy that she radiates also flows through her home. As someone who is obsessed with details, I definitely feel a kindred spirit in Brandy—from how every item in her home is so thoughtfully arranged to how organically yet technically placed each arch and ending point is marked in her calligraphy. She's a thinker and a feeler like me, balancing artistry with structure within her space and her work. I see those two sides of her expressed so vibrantly in her home—and especially in her living room. There is a subtle structured grid repeated throughout the room, from the arrangement of her furniture to the perfect square boxes of her golden shelf. But within those organized lines and grids are explosions of color and personality, the structure underneath allowing for more vibrancy and free visual expression above. It's that composure and grounded but warm spirit within both her home and her that I love. Brandy is a beautiful example of how to invest in your home to inspire pride and joy in who you are.

BRANDY'S LIVING ROOM

Brandy truly knows how to live in her own skin. Her totally approachable, warm, and down-to-earth vibe is not the least bit out of sync with her overtly feminine style of dressing, from her girlie dresses to her glam coral lipstick. And both her love of the rustic Pacific Northwest she grew up in and her attraction to refined elegance are most evident in her living room or, as she likes to call it, "the parlor" or "the cocktail room." Step in, and you'll immediately get what this room is all about—and why it's the best representation of who she is and how she presents herself to the world, from her own family of three and her extended family to friends and neighbors.

No matter how refined Brandy's home might strike you at first look, nothing is off-limits—not to be touched or used well.

She grew up with those kinds of strict rules and furniture you weren't supposed to actually *sit* on, and while she wants to live surrounded by the beautiful things she so coveted as a child, she also wants them to be enjoyed by her family, her friends, and herself.

Anchored by a chic but comfortably lived-in tufted velvet sofa in a soft shade between gray and mauve and refinished hardwood floors, Brandy's living room achieves a rare balance between a delicate lightness and genuine comfort. Your eye is drawn to the large, gold-framed abstract art above her white mantel—a study in fuchsia, oranges, and yellows—made by Minted designer Kelli Hall. (She is a huge supporter of local and independent artists.) Other pops of gold, as well as pinks and greens, run throughout, including on the gilded mirrors that she

collects, on the legs of a lamp, and on a salvaged glass shelving unit that she outlined in gold with spray paint. But those elegant elements are juxtaposed against more earthy ones like a deep-chestnut cowhide on the floor and a shelf that displays framed photographs of her family, favorite books, and found objects like geodes and coral. Perhaps the best example of this dichotomy is on her coffee table, where a lovely bouquet of white hydrangeas that would fit in at a high-end wedding sits next to a commonplace pack of playing cards (Brandy is known to play a mean game of gin rummy at any given moment). One half of the room brings the couch, chairs, and coffee table close together to invite intimacy, while the other half allows space for entertaining and a gorgeous rolling, wooden bar cart (an antique she amazingly got for twenty dollars) and French doors that look out onto a big deck and the towering cedar trees beyond.

HOW BRANDY'S LIVING ROOM FOSTERS COMMUNITY

It's really how she and her family live in the space that underscores the balance of chic and cozy. Brandy loves to host parties, particularly dance parties, and that extra space near the vintage bar cart with its gold cocktail tools quickly transforms into a kind of stage when the time is right. "We are definitely the liveliest neighbors," she says. During the holidays, she outfits her parlor with a massive Christmas tree and hosts her big extended family and closest friends for dinner. "People just get an inviting, laid-back vibe but also appreciate the aesthetic of our home. We love having family nearby and the sound of a full house. During the warmer months we leave the French doors open to enjoy the surrounding greenbelt." Brandy has a sophisticated home that's also fun and functional for her daughter. They've had roller-skate, jump-rope, and hula-hoop contests indoors! At Christmas her little family of three piles onto the velvet couch and cuddles by the fire. It's that willingness to allow beauty and good times to coexist that makes Brandy's home so unique. However, when it's not the setting for parties or impromptu sleepovers, her living room is the most quiet, purposeful room in the house, and that change in function echoes the duality of refinement and casualness in the décor. There's a motto hanging at the entrance that reads: "No Whining. No Complaining." Instead, it's all lightheartedness: think cocktails and card games, music and art. Nature is present throughout the room in both rustic and luxe ways as well, via antlers on the wall and small vases filled with flowers and little plants.

"We do pretty much everything in this room, from folding clothes to dancing, but on a beautiful day, I open the windows and listen to the birds while sketching or reading."

Ultimately, she wants people to feel comfortable when they come to visit, because as she says: What's a home if it's not enjoyed by friends and family? But it's just as important that *she* feels comfy there too. "We do pretty much everything in this room, from folding clothes to dancing, but on a beautiful day, I open up the windows and listen to the birds while sketching or reading."

A HOUSE WITH HISTORY

It's interesting that Brandy has such a love for antique and heirloom pieces considering that her home was formerly her in-laws'

and her husband grew up there. Though it had lots of dark wood and was very English manor–like when they first moved in, she's slowly been brightening it up. From having the floors restored to their original white oak to painting the fireplace and mantel white, she approaches the home one thing at a time. "I try to work with whatever I have and just put my spin on it. I like clean lines, simple shapes, and natural elements—playfulness is the base of my design. French provincial accessories add pops of lightness, like the nineteenth-century reclaimed mirrors." And while you can't deny the thoughtful elegance of Brandy's home, its seeming perfection is a bit of a trick. "The sofa was a gift from my mother and I love it. She taught me that if you buy quality pieces, they'll last a lot longer." But then, "These," she says, pointing to rattan chairs, "my husband purchased at a yard sale. When the weaving started to unravel, I threw a sheepskin over it. So be careful if you see sheepskin somewhere in my house! I can't let things go. I love that heirloom quality. Anything in my house, I'm keeping it forever. I'm secretly eighty-five." Over time she hopes to have all the things she desires. Until then, she'll just keep chipping away at her springboard and DIYing as much as she can. On achieving that balance of refinement and playfulness, she adds: "That's definitely who I am. I will find something in a bin in an antique store and polish it up the best I can and put it on my shelf—mixed with vintage family photos, books from my husband's 103-year-old grandmother, and pieces from flea markets, estate sales, and modern boutiques."

TAXIDERMY ART

THE flower WORKSHOP

PAPER TO PETAL   REBECCA THUSS and PATRICK FARRELL

A PRIVILEGED LIFE   ASSOULINE

JEAN-MICHEL BASQUIAT   TASCHEN

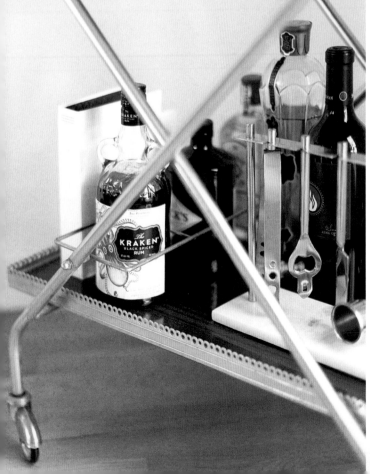

KRAKEN
BLACK SPICED
RUM

BRANDY'S TIPS

for Imbuing a Space with Elegance and Whimsy

The trick to creating liveliness and fun within a refined space is figuring out how to control and organize vignettes with various purposes. Brandy knows all the tricks for making a chic room an open playground for any purpose and mood. Whether you want to add more sophistication to a room that often feels cluttered or invite more engagement in a space that feels too sterile, here are some tips for balancing elegance and whimsy with ease.

- Add practicality—there's nothing in here that I don't use, haven't read, or don't adore, from pictures of my mom and dad and uncle when they were kids to decks of cards.

- Use art as color. If you can throw art anywhere, do it. It speaks volumes to a room and who you are and what you like—whether it's a splurge or a piece you find online or from a local artist in your community.

- Keep clean lines and use symmetry (e.g., two of the same chairs or throw pillows, books grouped on a shelf by color).

- Get loose within controlled spaces. For instance, keep walls neutral but layer patterns via artwork and textiles. Even though I do a lot of gold, I still mix metals, like silver and gold.

- Make spray paint your friend. So many of my gold accents are about me and a can of paint.

Kitchen

Finding Peace in Process

THE KITCHEN HAS ALWAYS BEEN MY most challenging room. Cooking for fun has never interested me and I get really impatient doing it. I've cooked chicken one time in my life, gave myself food poisoning in the process, and haven't cooked meat since. That was in 2013! Though I'm a perpetually hungry woman, always anticipating my next meal or snack, I despise cooking and food prep. My anxiety rises sometimes to the point where I make myself sick by the time I've finished cooking a meal. I'm not even kidding. But do I still want to learn how to cook? Yes!

Over the years, I've definitely put a lot of everyday life skills, like cooking, on hold in order to achieve major career goals at a young age. But now that I've entered my thirties, I'm realizing that I feel far behind many of my peers when it comes to essential practical matters—like cooking, planning for a family, or buying a home. Women around my age, and within progressive circles as far back as the 1980s, have been told, "You can have it all! A powerful career, domestic bliss—it's all attainable at once!" But how many of us have actually been taught real skills to find success in both our career and home life? For me, perfection in either category is not only impossible but actually not even desirable. It's the journey, the learning, and the accumulation of new experiences that bring me true satisfaction, pride, and joy. It just takes trusting my intuition and finding comfort within uncomfortable situations (like in my kitchen!) to make it happen.

An experience I had my freshman year of college really solidified my understanding of this—how I need room to not only grow as I pursue challenges but also enjoy the pursuit along the way. At a freshmen mixer, I was sitting with a group of other eighteen-year-olds and we each were given a little slip of paper with a question to answer and share with everyone. Mine said: "If you could be the best at anything, what would it be?" My response was: "I don't want to be the best at anything. Once you've become the best, where is there to go? I like seeing new opportunity for achievement and being 'the best' takes away that joy." My peers laughed, which initially made me feel bad and set the tone for a difficult year ahead. But, ultimately, in verbalizing that thought, it lead me on a journey of realizing what I needed to feel fulfilled, and in turn, I transferred schools, found community that supported me, and found confidence in my voice, my goals, and my understanding of self. One moment or one statement can sometimes magically help you discover what you truly need to thrive. That moment taught me that I find nourishment in *process*, fulfillment in the opportunity for growth and learning.

For me, progress has come much more naturally within the work realm. Progress in domestic skills has been something I've not only neglected my whole life but shunned as antithetical to my identity. But now that I'm thirty-one, I'm married, and I have health problems that need nurturing, I suddenly realize that a home ec class in high school could have helped better prepare me for adulthood. No matter how outside the mold my life is, or how much I reject society's dictation of gender roles, I still need to feed myself, take care of my health, and cultivate a home that brings me peace and wellness. And I'm finally ready to learn.

Of any room in my home, the kitchen is obviously the area most rooted in nourishment and practice. Now, the first step is just feeling comfortable in the actual space! As is true for any part of my home and my office, when I don't see a reflection of myself in it, I don't feel right. Unfortunately, though, the design of my kitchen doesn't offer much room for me to add my personal touch to it. Don't get me wrong: it's a beautiful kitchen, remodeled by the former owner to reflect the home's modern and midcentury modern vibe. But when it comes to infusing *my* style into it, there is literally no wall space where I can decorate or add art. I'm already intimidated by cooking, so not being able to visualize myself in my kitchen adds another layer of discomfort. But, true to my credo of embracing process and growth, that inability to really customize our kitchen was in itself inspiration for me to create something semipermanent within our space that not only reflects my aesthetic but also encourages me to engage with my kitchen and cooking. My Herb Drying Rack (page 38) has quickly become my favorite thing in my kitchen, encouraging me to experiment with flavor with less fear as I cook. I have an awful memory, especially when it comes to taste, so seeing visual reminders of flavors every day as herbs hang in my kitchen helps me to recall meals I have made and enjoyed, ones that I want to try again and again. Seeing visual reminders of inspiration for experimentation in the kitchen

has become my greatest asset in finding growth through cooking. And the more flavors I can add into my meals, the more I know my body and health will thrive.

Beyond a desire for constant personal growth, my health requires that investment. My physical and mental health have been challenges for me throughout my life. I recognized I was depressed at a very young age, was diagnosed with ADD at age six, and have had allergies of all kinds since I was a baby. My lifelong battle with depression and anxiety and my allergies to the world around me have only increased with time. In my early twenties, I became *somewhat* comfortable in my kitchen cooking for just one. But right after my twenty-fourth birthday, I began to have allergic reactions to all pitted fruits, wheat, and a few other delicious things. Since childhood, I'd been a great eater. But when I suddenly began reacting to things I ate regularly, I became fearful, not knowing what was going to potentially trigger a reaction. Some days were fine, but other days my mouth, lips, and throat would throb, itch, and swell after I ate an avocado or a strawberry, and I'd feel sick to my stomach and super bloated. I was living off my little Etsy shop at the time and I couldn't even fit a coffee from a coffee shop into my budget, so I put off going to an allergist. But when I started having allergic reactions to the free Craigslist couch my husband got for our living room when we first moved in together, it was definitely time to get things figured out. At twenty-seven, I finally was diagnosed with allergies to all trees, all grasses and weeds, all animal dander, almost all metals and dust mites, but no food! Essentially, my allergies to the outdoors and indoors were triggering reactions to foods because my immune system was beat up from just trying to survive everyday life. I didn't know the sort of support I needed to provide for my body, and only recently did I figure out what health and wellness means for me.

Thanks to inspiring women and friends like Mickey Trescott, the author of *The Autoimmune Paleo Cookbook* and *The Autoimmune Wellness Handbook*, and Devyn Elliott, a nutritional therapy practitioner, I've learned a lot in the last year about how to heal my gut and combat my autoimmune problems. But it's still scary for me, facing the kitchen head-on. I'm slowly learning how to create dishes that don't require too much fuss like enchiladas, tacos, and empanadas. Any food that is surrounded by bread, dough, or a tortilla is my kind of meal, self-contained and comforting. But on days when my allergies are bad, I usually focus on eating raw veggies, proteins, and smoothies, things that are easy to pull together and gentle on my stomach.

Everyone has something that holds them back even in the face of great possibilities and positive outcomes, whether it's the fear of cooking, fear of completing a project, or the broader fear of the unknown. But the journey toward that fear is still worth each step you take—and yes, that includes the failures and missteps too. In my career, I've tested new avenues and ditched others, experimented and taught myself a lot, and failed plenty. I've been a musician, a graphic designer, an illustrator, a blogger, a retail-store owner, a jewelry designer, and an author, and I've done plenty of other jobs like nannying, house cleaning, welding, artist assisting, clerical working, and so much more. Trying it all has been the name of my game. Because I just let it all happen and enjoyed the process of exploring, even during tears and hardships, I've gotten to the place where I am today. Allowing fear to be present in that journey, while not letting it hold me back in tackling challenges, has been the secret to my personal and career success, and I know I've got it in me to apply that spirit to how I feel in my kitchen as well!

When it comes to decorating, so many of us have an aversion to commitment—the idea that if you invest in something but end up hating it, it's a waste of your time and money. In cooking, I fear commitment because I'm worried that I will waste time, money, and food by making a meal that I won't like or that I'll ruin. But how can I figure out what I do enjoy cooking if I don't even try? Just like experimenting with style, experimenting with flavor is a worthy challenge. So my goal in my kitchen has been to combat that fear of inefficiency by trying out new and easy-to-follow recipes, buying things like herb plants that are quite literally an investment in me and my family since they can be used in our daily meals, and by purchasing beautiful kitchen utensils. I love copper, so I've collected items that are made with this material: a teapot, a pepper grinder, a fruit bowl, measuring cups, a tea strainer, and even a dish drying rack! Since there is little room to decorate, I've focused on investing in attractive kitchen essentials instead of traditional décor like art. I started hunting thrift stores for interesting trays, tins, and useful brass and copper knickknacks to get my collection going. And once I decided copper was the color I liked most in my kitchen, I started searching out newer copper kitchen items on eBay and Amazon. All the warm, glowing copper found in my kitchen tools and containers helps draw my artistic eye to my kitchen, which in turn makes me happy and excited to use these lovely items in a space that normally makes me nervous.

At Home in Your Space

KITCHEN

What in your kitchen encourages you to grow, learn, and take simple risks? Whether your challenge is finding a creative way to decorate your space, discovering a meal that everyone in your family will love, or feeling self-assured that you won't burn your dinner again, the risk is worth the challenge. And discomfort is a lot easier to handle if you just change the word to anticipation or adventure. Just like I learned my freshman year of college, being the best isn't what brings me joy. It's the learning and experimenting that cultivates fulfillment and pride. What is the next new meal you want to experiment with in your kitchen, and what can you bring into your space to encourage yourself to spend more time there? I'll start with tea in my shiny copper pot and cookies on my favorite copper dish!

Consider your own space as you ponder these questions. Let your mind wander! Feel free to use the Notes section in the back of the book for journaling or sketching out ideas.

- What are some of your favorite foods from your childhood and present?

- Do you have the ingredients and equipment on hand and accessible to make your favorite meals?

- How do you like to keep track of what food you have in the house and what meals you want to try?

- Are the tools, dishes, and foods you use most accessible and easy to get to?

- What practical items that you already have might have decorative potential?

- What mood/vibe/feeling do you want your kitchen to have?

- What colors reflect that mood?

- What decorative items do you already have that connect to that mood?

Here are a few simple things that have worked for me to make the kitchen more inviting and help me get over the intimidation I feel in this room. I hope you can use them too—or that they'll spark other ideas for making your kitchen a place where you can find pleasure in the act of nourishment.

FIVE KITCHEN DECORATING TIPS
TO INSPIRE SELF-INVESTMENT

1 Use clear jars to organize pastas, grains, beans, rice—any dry goods you cook with often and want nearby when you are throwing a meal together. Whether they are tucked away in your cupboard or out on your counter, all of their contents look so much more beautiful and feel more accessible when you see them on display together.

2 Display your cookbooks on your counter or a shelf. Not only are they beautiful objects, but they challenge me to try new things in the kitchen. Sometimes I just pick one up and wind up on the sofa reading and poring through the beautiful photography, dreaming up menus for future dinner parties. It's part practical and part fantasy.

3 A fresh bouquet of flowers is an affordable way to bring new and colorful inspiration and life into any space. In the summer, blooms from my garden do the trick or get added to other arrangements. But I also buy from farmers' markets, Trader Joe's, and other grocery stores, where bouquets are usually ten dollars or under. Sometimes I'll take a larger bouquet and arrange it into two smaller ones. That way, I have one for the kitchen counter and one for the dining table.

4 Invest in a few decorative dining items that are practical for hosting parties and gatherings and look great on display in your home even if there isn't a party going down. I've found some really cool dining items like vintage Moroccan tea glasses, crystal decanters, and brass trays and bowls at thrift stores. They were all super affordable but make my kitchen feel really beautiful and elegant whether they are on display or being used.

5 Add a rug! Not many people keep a rug in their kitchen, but there's no reason not to, as a kitchen gets as much foot traffic as a living room usually does. Bring the warm and inviting spirit of a relaxing living room into your kitchen through a beautiful but durable rug to encourage comfort within your cooking space. Just be sure to place a nonskid mat underneath to keep it from slipping on smooth kitchen floors. And consider choosing a vibrant pattern to distract from any stains—something that can take a glass of wine or a splotch of jam without bringing you to tears. Avoid light colors or superdelicate fabrics.

Make: HERB DRYING RACK

My favorite parts of any meal are the herbs and sauces, the details that make a meal come to life. Most meals call for just a dash of herbs, so when picking herbs from your garden or buying fresh herb bundles from the grocery store, you can save all your extras and dry them here on your drying rack for later use! It's not only useful but decorative, and fills your kitchen with the scent of delicious dried herbs.

STEPS

1. Cut your twine into six pieces, each 15 inches long.

2. Create a small loop at the end of each piece of twine.

3. Take one piece of twine and, using the unlooped end, wrap it around the base of one bunch of herbs, tying it off tightly and leaving the loop exposed.

4. Repeat this process with each bunch of herbs.

5. Remove the inner hoop from the embroidery hoop. You won't be using the outer hoop, just the inner one.

6. Measure how far you would like your herb drying rack to hang from the ceiling. Take that measurement and add 10 inches. Now cut three pieces of twine to that length. I wanted mine to hang about 15 inches from the ceiling, so I cut three 25-inch pieces of twine.

7. Using about 5 inches of one piece of twine, wrap it a few times around the hoop, and tie off.

8. Repeat this process with the two other pieces of twine, making sure that the three pieces of twine are equal distances from each other.

9. String three wooden beads onto each of these pieces of twine.

10. Gather the loose ends of the three pieces of twine and tie them all together, leaving 5 inches between the knot and the end of each piece. Make sure that when you hold up the hoop by the twine, it looks balanced.

11. Create a loop with one of the 5-inch ends of twine. Using the superglue, glue the end of the loop to the base knot. Then wrap the two leftover 5-inch pieces of twine around the knot and glue the ends to the knot.

MATERIALS AND TOOLS

Baker's twine

Measuring tape

Scissors

6 bunches fresh herbs (you can find these at your local grocery store, usually in the vegetable section in little plastic packaging—I used oregano, rosemary, thyme, bay leaves, tarragon, and sage)

1 (14-inch) embroidery hoop

9 (25-millimeter) wooden beads

Superglue

6 clothespins

Ceiling hook

For information on where to buy materials and tools, see Resources (page 185).

12. Using the clothespins, evenly attach the herb bundles to the hoop by clipping the clothespind to the hoop and to the loop of twine on the end of each herb bundle.

13. Evenly space your clothespins around the hoop so the herb bundles are balanced.

14. Now, simply screw in a ceiling hook where you want to hang your herb drying rack, and hang it up!

Make: FLORAL ICE CUBES

This is one of the simplest ways to dress up a delicious drink, whether you are sharing cocktails with friends or wanting to add a little color and fun to a punch at a party. Not only do these ice cubes add a pop of color, but some of them will even subtly change the taste of a drink. Pick edible flowers from your own yard or garden or buy them at gourmet stores or from florists.

Most refrigerators and freezers have a temperature setting. Reduce your freezer temperature to help the ice cubes freeze more slowly, preventing the cubes from getting foggy.

STEPS

1. Boil the distilled water and then allow it to cool completely. It's very important to use distilled water that has also been boiled and then cooled so that the ice cubes are clear and not foggy.

2. Fill each tray cube one-third to halfway with the distilled water.

3. Add the flowers on top of water, then freeze.

4. Put the rest of your distilled water in the refrigerator to keep it cold (and prevent it from melting your previous layer of ice when applying it in the next step).

5. Once the first layer is frozen, fill each tray cube with cold distilled water and freeze again.

6. Add the cubes to a clear cocktail, water, or soda to draw all the attention to the colorful, tasty ice cubes!

MATERIALS AND TOOLS

1 gallon distilled water

Regular or large ice tray (the bigger the cubes, the slower the ice will melt, which is best!)

Edible flowers

For information on where to buy materials and tools, see Resources (page 185).

CHOOSING SAFE EDIBLE FLOWERS

Use only *edible* flowers. I love pansies since they come in lots of natural colors; lavender, which is yummy in lemonade; and rose teas that come simply as buds. Just make sure that whichever edible flower you choose has not been treated with chemicals: use flowers from your own garden or buy flowers that are labeled "organic" or "edible flowers." Keep it simple by choosing just a couple of flowers. Too many petals floating in a drink could get bothersome; the key is to make it pretty and subtle.

Edible flower options: pansies, lavender, rose petals, carnations, violets, chamomile flowers, citrus petals, English daisy, hibiscus, lilac, mint flowers, rosemary flowers, sage flowers, or sunflower petals.

LOOKING ON THE BRIGHT SIDE WITH
Diana La Counte

DIANA LA COUNTE

*Lifestyle blogger at OurCityLights.com,
creative director, and tech consultant*

LIVES IN: Anaheim, California

FROM: Fullerton, California

SIGNATURE STYLE: retro-inspired modern with
a touch of storybook fantasy

HOW SHE BECAME A BLOGGER: She started
out using LiveJournal as a form of journaling (I
did too!) back in the mid-2000s. Her artistic
eye in her former career as a cosmetologist,
her unique perspective as a comic-book lover
and self-professed tech nerd, and her honest
and vulnerable writing style have garnered her a
devoted following.

WHAT SHE LOVES: bright, saturated color
(especially pink); vintage appliances; pop art
like Hello Kitty rugs, Andy Warhol prints, donut
art, and *The Royal Tenenbaums* memorabilia;
books; her own photography that evokes
nostalgia for things close to her heart; fresh
flowers; her two tiny dogs with big personalities; Disneyland

I've had the privilege of knowing Diana for about seven years. When I first started my blog back in 2009, she was one of the first people who I connected with. It has been incredible to watch her creativity and extraordinary aesthetic blossom and grow, as well as to see how she has faced painful experiences with grace, patience, and trust in herself. Her ability to find humor and joy even amid the banal or the tragic is something I admire and relate to a lot. As the years have gone by, she and I have actually battled a few similar challenges.

Not only do we both feel uncomfortable in the kitchen; we also have similar autoimmune disorders where, sometimes, even food we adore can make us sick and actually harm our bodies. Her recently diagnosed autoimmune disorder (MTHFR mutation) was a major cause in her struggle to get pregnant with both of her children and may have been a factor in the stillbirth of her first child, her son. Diana and I both understand the fragility of life, the fragility of our bodies, and the necessity of investing in ourselves and in the present,

savoring every joyful moment we can—and finding humor even amid tragedy. We also understand that the sacred honoring of hardship and pain is not lost when you give yourself room to laugh, play, and still find ways to enjoy your life. Diana loves injecting playful elements of her passions into her spaces, from her *Royal Tenenbaums* gallery wall to her pink mailbox, pink porch, and pink roses growing outside of her home. I know Diana's radiance and joy are extra powerful because she truly understands life's ups and downs.

For both of us, the kitchen is a challenge to invest in and use on a daily basis, yet she has managed to inject all the most creative and humorous elements of herself into the space. She allows dark humor to come out to play beside the bubbly fun of bright pinks and Hello Kitty tchotchkes. There's both lightness and depth dancing side by side in her space and within her, something that I relate to and admire deeply.

DIANA'S KITCHEN

Diana's kitchen is truly one of a kind, a blend of kitsch and humor with chic modernism. Diana wasn't always a pink fanatic, though. "You know what's really funny, and people are going to probably be like, 'What is wrong with this woman?' but I would never wear pink. At cosmetology school, I had to wear an all-black uniform. Then I worked in a salon for ten years and had to wear all black. I still wear pretty much only black and white today!" She is just more comfortable wearing a simple and chic black-and-white palette, but she loves surrounding herself with colors in

her environment that bring her positivity and joy. She also admits to hating cooking, prepping food, and doing the dishes. So painting the old cupboards in her 1907 Craftsman home her favorite bright color made the space less intimidating and helped her to want to actually spend time in there. "I don't like—and it sounds like a very immature thing to say—but I don't like doing these adult things, and I could just easily ask my husband to do it all and he would, but that's not how our marriage works." So, she explains, the playful colors and Hello Kitty novelty items "make it a little more livable." There's also an art wall in homage to her love of the movie *The Royal Tenenbaums*, which reminds her of her own family. When they come to visit it becomes a conversation piece because everyone can relate to a character.

HOW DIANA'S KITCHEN REFLECTS HER LIFE

Though her parents bought her all things Hello Kitty, she actually didn't like the character all that much as a child. But as she got older and held on to a few of the Hello Kitty knickknacks of her youth, her appreciation grew for the joy and lightness they evoke. With some serious challenges in her life—including living with an autoimmune disorder that affects everything from what she eats to how she breathes, and the traumatic stillbirth of her first child, Mordecai Max—she came to appreciate the whimsy of all things Hello Kitty. "Everything in my life was so serious and hard, but I had my little stash of Hello Kitty stationery that brought me comfort and happiness." That first stationery set became the inspiration for her to imbue her kitchen

with playfulness, relieving her of some of the weight of her hardships.

Her daughter, Miko Rey, was born just around the time I finished writing this book, and Diana has so much to celebrate now with this new healthy and beautiful addition to her family! But that doesn't erase the pain from the loss of her son. She balances an understanding and acceptance of life and death on a level that many people her age have yet to comprehend. And it is because of this deep understanding of the fragility and beauty of life that she invests in bringing joy into her home through vibrant colors and artwork that is fun yet tells a story—sometimes with a touch of dark humor. "Considering everything that I've been through, I just want people to come in and say, 'OK, you've been through some tough stuff but your house doesn't feel like it . . . There's some joy in here.'" Diana truly understands life's yin and yang, the dark and the light. And she has the courage to express both sides online through her blog and within the beautiful space of her home.

The kitchen, with its bright-pink walls, is a reminder to invest in her health—and to nourish herself despite the limitations of her disease. "I have to be more prepared. If I go out to eat instead of cooking for myself one day, it's fine, but if it's every day and I'm not taking care of myself, then there's a really good chance that the kitchen becomes a complete disaster too. If it's a mess, it means I haven't prepped anything, I haven't cleaned up from the last time, I haven't put anything away—I'm treating the kitchen like garbage and I'm treating my body like garbage." And that just doesn't fly for this incredibly resilient woman and mother who believes that happiness is always achievable, no matter what life throws her way.

HOME SWEET HOME

DIANA'S TIPS
for Adding Joy and Humor to Your Home

One of the secrets of getting older is that we all still hold on to so many qualities of who we were as children, for better or for worse. In growing up, we expect that age equals sophistication and maturity and that, somehow, those qualities are more important than even the positive elements of our youthful selves. Let Diana give you some tips on how to add joy, playfulness, and a touch of humor to your home by tapping into those things that brought you joy as a child. What are the colors you loved as a kid, the oddities that caught your fancy, or the things that sparked your imagination? Translate the vibrancy within you to your living space around you!

• Pull out those childhood toys you loved most, the things that brought you joy and made you laugh at a young age.

• Purchase and display items that spark conversation, like something kooky and strange you found at a flea market or a poster of a band, artist, or movie you love.

• Use colorful frames against white walls to add playfulness and pop to any room.

• Paint a door an unexpected color to make it feel like you are walking into a creative space. It makes guests wonder, *What's in there?*

Dining Room

Celebrating Friendship and Family

FOR ME, NOTHING IS AS SATISFYING to the soul as connecting with people on a deep, personal level. Once you "find your tribe," those people who you can be yourself around and genuinely want to spend time with, it's time to invest in the spaces where you nurture these relationships. That's the sort of spirit I cultivate in my dining room—a place of gathering and celebration. Our dining room definitely proved to be the trickiest room in our house (besides the kitchen) to decorate, since there are doorways and entrances in every wall. However, it also makes for a room that can shift and change depending on how we use it. In the late fall and winter, the French doors stay closed as the Seattle rain nurtures our garden outside, and we pile our beautiful vintage table (actually a 150-year-old writing desk I scored on Craigslist for just seventy-five dollars!) high with delicious food—like pies and soup homemade by my husband, perfect for cold and cozy days spent with friends. Candles on the dining table and on shelves around the room also make for the coziest setting for holiday dinner parties and get-togethers.

Come summer, we open up all the doors and turn our dining room into an extension of our big deck. We sometimes even pull our dining table out onto the porch for dinner to enjoy the warm evenings and late sunsets and so there is more room for mixing and mingling, making music together, or dancing as we sip cocktails late into the night. I found a really cool brass cabinet at Goodwill and managed to snag it for just fifty dollars; it makes the perfect bar and display for all the vintage knickknacks and beautiful glassware that I have found over the years at thrift stores. I don't drink very much, but I grew up loving the look of my dad's Craftsman-style antique cabinet that held all of his liquors, reserved for special occasions and parties, in antique decanters. I've tried to re-create that look that I admired in my parents' formal dining room within my brass and glass cabinet. But I've made it a little more modern, casual, and approachable with rustic handmade pots (also found at thrift stores), antlers, and plants to better suit our folksier, bohemian style.

To me, our dining room feels like a space for collecting and celebrating curious finds from random places just as much as it feels like a spot to enjoy and revel in the incredible friends and community my husband, my sister (who also lives with us), and I have gathered. I was very shy for most of my life, so finding a community of friends with common mind-sets and similar likes and dislikes was really hard from an early age, especially after I moved from a rural village in England to a mountain town the United States when I was eight. I'm lucky to have found a few friends in junior high and high school who took me in, though I was definitely a bit out-there, more liberal, artistic, and kooky than they. But our common understanding of how we wanted to be treated, respected, and loved despite any of our dissimilarities was what unified us. I'm lucky to call those women some of my favorite people today, though I live states away from most of them and see them only once a year if I'm lucky. They were the first peers who taught me that it's OK to be different, to stand out, and that it's possible to find deep and lifelong friendships despite differences in backgrounds, lifestyles, political leanings, and interests.

Though I had these beautiful, supportive relationships during some of the hardest years of my life in middle school and high school, I still craved new and different friendships and mentors in college. I think that desire came partly because I was so shy, and partly because I grew up in an isolated town in the Northern California mountains and was desperate for cultures, experiences, and lifestyles that related more to my own. After a tough freshman year of not fitting in at the college I chose, I decided to make a leap and moved to Seattle to transfer colleges. I had never even been to Washington, but I just trusted my gut and went for it. After my mom drove me up to my new campus on a fourteen-hour journey, dropped me off, and headed straight back to California, I realized, *OK, now is my time to start completely fresh*. I decided to make a shift in how I presented myself to others. To combat my insecurities, I practiced pretending to be outgoing even when I felt shy or like an outsider. At the end of the day, most people are more self-conscious and less interested in judging you than you realize, so I decided to be a source of positivity and kindness to the people I met at my new school, knowing we all have the same worries about fitting in.

It was there that I truly felt like I found peers who had not only similar ethics but also kindred rebellious spirits balanced with rational minds. My best friends in college were able to bring out a more playful and joyful spirit in me that I hadn't felt in a long time since moving to the United States. With my friends' encouragement, I became confident enough in my own music that I'd been

writing since I was fifteen to start performing publicly, and I even recorded an album at nineteen. It truly felt like one of the first times that I connected with lots of friends on every level, from surface interests to deeper bonds.

Then, right after I graduated college, blogging was the last frontier of finding people who I connected with deeply. I started my blog in 2009 and used it as a public space for journaling, a way to connect with niche communities far and wide that I couldn't find—or at least didn't know how to find—where I lived. From seeking out more girlfriends who liked shoegaze, jangle pop, pysch folk, music from the seventies, and noise rock like I did, to wanting to connect with other women who also had huge, creative career aspirations, blogging was where I found my group of badass independent women looking to find meaning and community through their creative pursuits. Through blogging I became comfortable with the words "spirit sisters" because it was via the internet that I found the women I could trade deep stories with—often, reading many of their stories ended with me exclaiming to myself, "Wow, me too!"

As I've traveled over the years for work and for pleasure, I've gotten to meet so many of my blogging friends in person, and if I loved them through online communication, every time I've met one of them in real life I've adored them even more. Many of those friends are profiled here within this book. One of my friends who I met through blogging eventually moved to Seattle many years after we first connected online, and upon meeting in person for the first time in my store, we knew within seconds that we'd be best friends. When I get the chance to host some of my friends in my home, whether they are friends I've met through blogging, visiting from far and wide, or Seattle locals, I am beyond overjoyed. My husband and I both share this love for hosting friends: he shares his love for community through cooking and I share mine through storytelling and games. Exchanging tales over the dinner table with mood lighting glowing overhead, laughter echoing throughout, and the sun setting outside our big French doors is our absolute favorite time at home.

Perhaps the greatest thing about community is how you have a lifetime to develop it. There is space to let go of some people when your paths diverge, room to develop new relationships and bring others in, and opportunity to rediscover old friendships and start new bonds. The unique ways and places in which I've made friendships inspires how I decorate the dining room, the physical space where I host these wonderful people. I love the classic and vintage pieces that ground the room, like our dining table, midcentury modern–style chairs, and the print of a painted portrait of a woman that my dad bought for me when I was six years old and we visited a museum together for the first time. The history, solidity, and sturdiness of those larger pieces reflect to me the steadfast love and personal investment of family and friends. And the lighter pieces, the detailed bits and baubles in our vintage brass cabinet, the pale bohemian wall décor made by artists within my community and the objects on our tabletop that change with the seasons (or whatever party we are hosting) reflect the eclectic group of friends we have gathered. Now that I'm in my thirties, a few friends from our childhoods (did I mention my husband and I grew up in neighboring small towns?) have found their way up to Seattle. Meanwhile, friends from college here in Seattle have spread across the world. And those real-life connections with so many women I've met through blogging? A few of them have moved near me from other states and have become real-life best friends. I feel so lucky to have this community!

Though I am not much of a planner or the best at cleaning, having a dining room I love is a great motivation to host a gathering, dinner, game night, or cocktail party at my home, which, in turn, is also an inspiration to really invest in my space by cleaning and tidying in preparation for friends to visit. Just like I dress myself, take a shower, and eat a good breakfast every day out of respect for myself, I want to treat my home, particularly my dining room, with that same love. Decorating a space where friends can gather easily, no matter if it's big or small, fancy or simple, is a lovely way to welcome your community into your home. Nourishment goes beyond just delicious food; to fill yourself with the presence of your friends and family is the greatest gift you can give yourself—and the dining room is where my heart feels its fullest, soaking in the love of the people closest to me.

At Home in Your Space

DINING ROOM

How does your dining room or area where you commune over food and drink nurture friendships? Maybe your dining table has an extendable leaf that offers more room for lots of guests, or you have a beautiful display of cocktail bits and baubles that makes drinks with friends not only tastier but beautiful too. Perhaps you collect vintage china or glassware in a rainbow of colors that liven up your tabletop, or you decorate with seasonal pieces or style a floral centerpiece to complement the colors of the food you serve at dinner. There are so many ways to share who you are in this space while making others feel thoroughly at home. Look around you: there might be a piece of furniture that simply needs a sanding and a coat of paint or fresh stain, walls that could use a different color, or a piece of art that's been hiding in your closet, begging for a frame. On the flip side, you might already have the perfect essentials and just need a trip to a flea market or Target to buy some décor with a pop of color or metallic accents to liven up the room. Take stock of what you already have in your dining room, and fill in the gaps with unique objects that encourage friends old and new to feel their most comfortable and welcomed in your home.

Consider your own space as you ponder these questions. Let your mind wander! Feel free to use the Notes section in the back of the book for journaling or sketching out ideas.

- Where do you like to eat in your home? Is your dining space separate, in your kitchen, or do you like to eat in your living room? How can you make your eating space special?

- What are some of your favorite memories of sharing meals with people you love?

- What is your favorite size gathering? Do you prefer to connect with friends and family individually or do you love the energy of large gatherings? How many people do you want your dining space to hold?

- What mood/vibe/feeling do you want your dining room to have?

- What colors reflect that mood?

- What decorative items do you already have that connect to that mood?

Whether you've never hosted a dinner party or, like me, you love welcoming friends for dinner, there are always new ways to make dinner parties more relaxed, fun, and memorable. Here are my top tips for introducing new friends, utilizing your space, and creating a magical evening!

TEN TIPS FOR HOSTING AN AFFORDABLE, BEAUTIFUL, AND MEMORABLE DINNER PARTY

1   Hunt thrift stores for a mix of fun plates and glassware. You can find a huge assortment of formal crystal glassware, decanters, and unique plates at thrift stores that cost little but offer a cool and eclectic visual impact when mixed and mismatched on a dining table.

2   Don't worry about mixing store-bought food with homemade when planning your menu. Don't feel like you have to hand-make every little thing. Mostly people just want to hang out with you!

3   Use a paint pen to write guests' names on leaves and use the leaves as place cards for guests to find their seats at the table.

4   Light a few unscented candles around your home before friends come over and add a few to your dining table. No matter how styled your home is or isn't, candles can really fill a space once the lights are dimmed and the sun goes down, bringing life and warmth into any space. And unscented candles won't steal the show from your delicious-smelling food.

5   Have an intimate dinner where you introduce a few friends who you think would really click and have complementary personalities. Instead of introducing people as "Jane, who is a teacher," introduce each person with their name and how they are special to you as well as something they might have in common with someone else at your dinner party.

6 Make a signature cocktail for hangout time before you start dinner, something that reflects your personality and personal taste!

7 Utilize the entire space of your home for hosting friends for dinner. Start in the living room with a cocktail and light snacks, an easy way to get people comfortable. Move to the dining table for dinner. And after dinner, move to an outdoor space in the summer or a cozy spot in your home for games and dessert in winter. Why not make a full night of it?

8 Make extra dessert and send guests home with a to-go box.

9 Add a fun surprise to the end of your evening. My husband built a mini fire pit in our backyard for roasting marshmallows with friends or talking over the fire before they head home. You can also throw a dance party, play old records on a record player, play games, or watch a funny or nostalgic movie that everyone loves.

10 Create a printout of any special recipes from your meal for guests to take home and use later.

Make: GOLD-PATTERNED GLASSWARE

Gold-patterned glassware can oftentimes cost upwards of fifty dollars a glass! Yikes. Here is a simple way to create an elegant, quirky, and unique set for your next party on a budget. I decided to use whiskey glasses and a decanter rather than wineglasses or champagne flutes because I like the more masculine aesthetic. Grab a couple of highball glasses from your local thrift store, Ikea, or Target, and let's get fancy!

STEPS

1. Wash the glassware with soap and water.

2. Wet a paper towel with rubbing alcohol and wipe off any oils, fingerprints, or soap residue, and let dry for 7 minutes.

3. Use tape to create clean lines that you can follow with the Sharpie. Check out my examples (see the opposite page) for some inspiration. If you want to create your own designs, bear in mind that geometric designs work well. Or freehand draw your designs! If you mess up, don't worry! Use rubbing alcohol to clean up your mistakes and start over.

4. Air-dry your designs for 24 hours. Oil-based paints take a long time to dry.

5. After your designs have dried, line a baking sheet with foil and place the glasses on the sheet.

6. Place the baking sheet with the glasses on it in an unheated oven.

7. With the baking sheet and glasses in the oven, preheat the oven to 350 degrees F, and start a timer for 20 minutes as soon as you start the preheat.

8. After 20 minutes, turn off the oven and leave the glassware in for 10 more minutes with the door closed while the oven cools down.

9. Open the oven door. Remove the baking sheet but let the glasses cool for about 15 more minutes before handling them. They will be hot!

10. When the glasses are fully cooled, wash before using.

MATERIALS AND TOOLS

Glassware

Dish soap and water

Paper towels

Rubbing alcohol

Painter's tape

Sharpie Oil-Based Extra-Fine-Point Gold Paint Marker

Baking sheet

Aluminum foil

Oven

For information on where to buy materials and tools, see Resources (page 185).

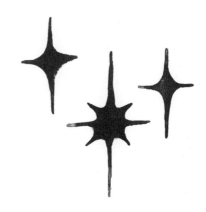

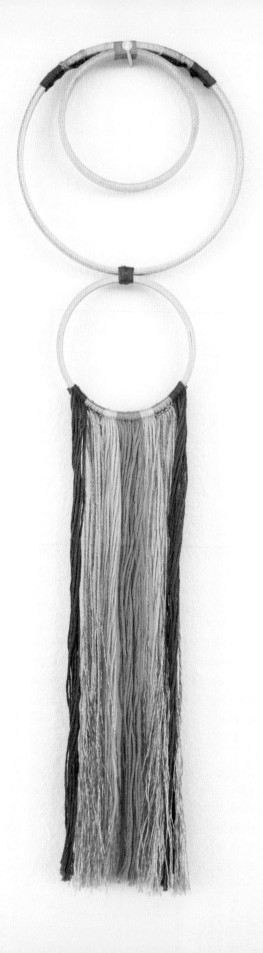

Make: MACRAMÉ WALL HANGING

Strike a balance between boho and femme with this simple wood-and-string wall hanging. And with no complicated knotting techniques, it should be a breeze to create!

STEPS

1. Start with one skein of each color floss. Cut the Golden Orange embroidery floss into eleven pieces of 24 inches. Cut the Light Grey into twelve pieces of 24 inches. Cut the Satin Blue into twelve pieces of 24 inches. Cut the Dark Turquoise into twelve pieces of 24 inches.

2. Attach your first piece of Golden Orange embroidery floss to one of the 3-inch hoops by folding the floss in half and aligning the two ends evenly. Then take the loop end of the floss and place it under the hoop. Bring the loop up over the hoop and string the two loose ends of the floss through the loop, then pull the two ends through and tighten the knot you have just created to the hoop edge. [see diagram on the following page]

3. Repeat step 2 ten more times with the Golden Orange floss, each time keeping the floss very tight together as you add more along the hoop.

4. Take six of the Light Grey pieces of floss and add them to the left side of the Golden Orange floss on the hoop. Repeat this step with six more Light Grey pieces on the other side of the Golden Orange floss.

5. Repeat step 4 with the Satin Blue floss, adding six pieces on the left and six on the right side of the Light Grey. Satin floss can be really slippery. If the knot isn't staying closed, take the two ends of the string and pull a regular tight knot into place at the same spot as the previous knot. [see diagram on the following page]

6. Repeat step 4 with the Dark Turquoise floss, adding six pieces on the left and six on the right side of the Satin Blue.

. . . *continued*

MATERIALS AND TOOLS

2 skeins each of 4 different embroidery floss colors (I used Golden Orange 976, Light Grey 648, Satin Blue S414, and Dark Turquoise 924 from the brand DMC)

Scissors

2 (3-inch) embroidery hoops

1 (5-inch) embroidery hoop

Superglue

Nail

For information on where to buy materials and tools, see Resources (page 185).

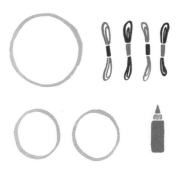

7. From your second skein of Dark Turquoise, cut a 24-inch piece. Use this piece to attach the 3-inch hoop you've been working on to the 5-inch hoop. Wrap it around both hoops once [see diagram], then tie a tight knot in the back. Wrap the rest of the floss around the two hoops over and over, pulling tightly. Then, when there is about 2 to 3 inches left on each end, tie them together a few times in the back and cut off the excess floss. Add a drop or two of glue to the knot so it stays in place.

8. Cut a 24-inch piece of Golden Orange from your second skein. Use this to attach the second 3-inch hoop to the top of your 5-inch hoop, inside it, following the method in step 7. [see diagram]

9. Cut two 24-inch pieces of floss from each of the remaining three unopened skeins of Light Grey, Satin Blue, and Dark Turquoise.

10. Wrap one piece of the Light Grey tightly around just the top of the 5-inch hoop, to the left of the Golden Orange wrap, and tie it off in the back. Repeat this on the right side of the Golden Orange with the second piece of Light Grey floss. [see diagram]

11. Repeat step 10 with the two Satin Blue floss pieces and the two Dark Turquoise pieces.

12. Add a drop or two of superglue to each of the knots on the back of each wrapped color along the 5-inch hoop so the knots stay in place.

13. Check out the bottom of your embroidery floss tassels and feel free to trim any pieces that look a little too long. Gently smooth out the floss with your hands.

14. Add a nail to your wall and simply rest the top hoop on the nail to add a touch of rustic, quirky charm to your space!

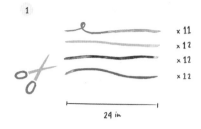

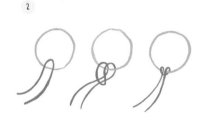

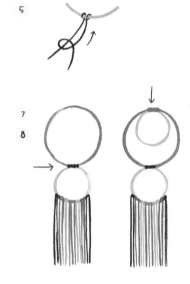

COLLECTED TREASURES WITH
Brooke Eide

BROOKE EIDE

Interior designer, graphic designer, and Craigslist curator

LIVES IN: Seattle, Washington

FROM: Cleburne, Texas

SIGNATURE STYLE: modern bohemian eclectic meets folksy Texas ranch

WHAT SHE LOVES: patterns and textiles, like saddle blankets and animal hides; natural items that evoke special memories, including pressed flowers from walks around her neighborhood; plants, like cactuses from the Texan landscape and her current favorite, fiddle leaf fig; intentional small pieces with stories behind them, be it a family heirloom or a Goodwill find; natural wood; copper; fiber art; repurposing unexpected things, like an old army cot draped with white fur as a bookend to her bed

WHERE SHE FINDS INSPIRATION: From her grandmother "Fonchie," her family full of artists, and her travels. "You go to places, like a restaurant, and you like that shade of blue, or you go to someone's house and see something interesting. If you see something you like, go for it! Don't be afraid to try something new and put your own stamp on it." Craigslist is a huge inspiration as well. In fact, she started *The Venatory*, a website and blog where she curates the hidden treasures she finds there. A serial Craigslist hunter, Brooke scours its depths daily to source the best products that the average browser may not notice at first glance. She then presents her finds on her website with better imagery, and she pairs rare finds and vintage wonders with new, fresh, and modern accessories from stores like West Elm and Ikea and unique handmade designers she admires.

If there is anyone's personal aesthetic that I envy, it has to be Brooke Eide's. Brooke is the cofounder of Flint, a design studio, where she, along with her husband and team, work on creating custom brands. They work on the needs of restaurants, retailers, and larger company clients from Seattle all the way to Seoul, Korea. She also runs her own interior design company, Fonchie Design, focused on residential clients and small companies, collaborating with stores like West Elm and Room & Board. I first discovered Brooke through Instagram a few years ago when she was living in San Francisco. The stars must have been aligned, as I later found out that I went to college—and had many art and design classes—with her best friend. Even

"If you see something you like, go for it! Don't be afraid to try something new and put your own stamp on it."

crazier, a few years later, Brooke ended up moving to Seattle and marrying her husband, Tyler, who also went to college and had shared a few art classes with me, and whose band played some of the same venues where I also performed my own music in college. Our many connections (one being that Marissa, the photographer of this book, was a friend of mine from college and also a neighbor and close friend of Brooke's) are so funny to me because they reflect our common love of celebrating the people we love through how we live and how we decorate. In great design and art of any kind, it's really that story within the creation that infuses it with power, whether it's a long narrative or a simple spark of imagination. Brooke's home

is filled with art from her grandmother "Fonchie," who she named her own design business after, an eclectic artist and decorator much like Brooke herself. So many of the pieces in her home have these stories, like the desk she and her husband built together in their office, and the chandelier in her dining room, which was a collaboration with her friends at Triple Seven. And a discarded sculpture that one of her relatives viewed as flawed is now one of her favorite objects in her home, a personal celebration of beauty found in imperfection. It is through her family's artistic background and her incredible community of creative friends that she has curated a home that reflects the inspiration that "her people" have on her life. If there is a lesson that I want to learn from her influence, it's to invest in your community and your home with intention, respect, and adoration.

BROOKE'S DINING ROOM

Brooke's dining room combines a West Elm midcentury modern–style table and vintage chairs with an antique buffet (a seriously gorgeous Craigslist find!). The table has a leaf that she can put away when she needs more space for friends, and the marble top of the buffet is the perfect home for their favorite collection of cocktail mixings and homemade treats. The buffet and an Oriental rug give the room a dash of classical sophistication while plants bring in the down-to-earth elements of nature, and a formerly dingy white tapestry from the 1970s that she hand-dyed a vibrant blue provides a pop of color and texture. And, of course, no room in Brooke's home—a former mansion converted into apartments— is complete without those one-of-a-kind nooks filled with ephemera that highlight important parts of her life. In one corner sits a mini collection—a kind of homage to her grandfather—with a portrait of him from World War II, his glasses that she remembers him by, and a trophy of his, given to her by her parents. "I've always been someone who curates everything around me. From my clothes to my interior, I like to collect unique items that stand out to me. Some of the pieces of my wardrobe I even consider to be wearable art!" she says. "I like to mix things up with my decorating. In a way, you can compare it to preparing food. You want each bite to feel different—it should be a journey of flavors. So with decorating I recommend really trying to mix things up. Find what takes dominance in one area and then accessorize around it." To showcase small pieces without clutter, she mixes sizes and heights.

She also likes to work with her hands and loves taking classes to learn new skills, from ceramics to upholstery. (Her home is filled with her own homemade décor, from copper lamps and a reupholstered seventies daybed, to a desk she designed from scratch.)

Though she admits she struggled a bit combining clean midcentury furniture and fixtures with older

"Be true to yourself. Even if it's not perfect, if you love it, that will make others feel comfy too."

antique detailing, she ultimately thought it was a nice mix of references—the seventies with the tapestry, the regal 1800s era from the buffet, and the sleek World War II era via the table. "The colors of the woods match, and somehow it just works. You're not replicating one era—just like you wouldn't decorate only using items from one store. That's advice I'd give to everyone. Be true to yourself. Even if it's not perfect, if you love it, that will make others feel comfy too."

HOW SHE USES HER DINING ROOM

That adherence to comfortable imperfection is reflected in how she incorporates her dining room into her life. "We host a lot. Part of that is because we have the space to do it, but more than anything, it's because we love doing it. I like making our home a place we want to be in. We use a lot of lamps instead of overhead lights, which makes it more calming. We have Friday-night pizza nights, and we make homemade pizza, play Liar's Dice, and drink whiskey in our sweatpants." She says that this room, in particular, feels the most like her—relaxed but stylish and ready for a good time with friends.

ON FINDING HER TRIBE

Brooke moved to Seattle in 2011 from the Bay Area when she got engaged. "When I was living in San Francisco, my best friend was there. She was creative too and we adventured together, threw everything in the car and drove to the beach. I needed to find another creative girl, not to replace her, but to help me get out of my funk. I made friends with the photographer of this book, Marissa, who up until recently lived right across the street from me, and who went to college with Moorea and my husband, and she became my best friend here in Seattle. I've been putting myself out there more too lately. It's really important for creative women to help each other. So—especially since I'm married—I'm more intentional about getting together with people. Now that the sun is out, I'm like, 'Let's go grab a drink! Let's hang out.' I love Seattle now! I found my people."

BROOKE'S TIPS
for Thrifting on Craigslist

Craigslist can be a treasure trove and a bit of a hell hole to sift through in search of that perfect something that you can't find anywhere else. It's my personal favorite place to go to find antiques at affordable prices and to discover truly unique pieces of furniture and decorative items that would normally be scooped up in a second if you saw them at a thrift store. I found an amazing set of peacock chairs on Craigslist which hang out in my yard all summer long, but it took some hunting in the depths of Craigslist to score peacock chairs at an affordable price. If there is anyone I know who can guide you in the art of Craigslist hunting, it's Brooke. Take her tips and see what magical finds turn up in your local Craigslist that could transform your home from generic and uninspired to personal, detailed, and rich in history.

* Be patient.

* Don't be afraid to go wide. Start in the furniture section and type in "vintage" or "midcentury" or "brass."

* Don't discount the sellers who aren't savvy. Someone who knows what they're doing will have all the right keywords. Do look for those specific keywords like "midcentury," "gold," "crystal," and "antique." But also try searching straightforward descriptor words like "dresser," "cabinet," "art," and "object" because an old grandma might have something great but not know its value or why it's cool.

* Look for bulk materials too. In my Flint office, I have a huge marble conference table. I got the marble for free because a building in Pioneer Square in Seattle was giving it away—a fifty-five- by seventy-five-inch piece! I found a company to cut it.

* Hunt through older listings.

Office

Nurturing Professional Growth

I PROBABLY SPEND MORE TIME IN my Seattle store's headquarters than anywhere else, including my own home! Because I founded my own company, my office there (which I share with my staff) is a reflection of who I am and what I care about most. But it took me a long time to really invest in decorating it to reflect not only my personal vibe but the inspiration and motivation behind my brand because, well, quite simply, business is busy! Whether you're a badass lady boss whose office is in the top of a skyscraper or an equally creative and determined woman who sets up a work space in a corner of your guest room or dining room, the office is such an important space in identifying what motivates you and inspires you in your professional pursuits. I think the common struggle of any woman is that we all juggle a lot of hats as we grow older and pursue our goals in work, home life, and creative or artistic endeavors. And remembering to invest in the spaces where we work to fulfill those goals can be a challenge, one that I know well. When decorating my offices at my store, I wanted a few things to shine through in this function-focused space: namely, the inspiration for why I founded an online retail site and a storefront and the reason why I taught myself jewelry making and started a blog back in 2009.

To spark visual inspiration based on what my team and I care about most, I created a gallery of art inspired and designed by women that hangs above our desks. I chose artwork that I've spotted across Pinterest, blogs, and Etsy to adorn our 90 percent woman-powered company, and the works themselves celebrate women and our uniqueness—like the quirky boob print by Maja Dlugolecki that's an homage to ladies of all shapes and sizes. There is so much pressure for women to look a certain way, particularly in the fashion industry, and to me, this piece of art celebrates the beauty of imperfection and diversity. I like

Moorea
Seal
Gets
What She
Wants

positive
vibes

to inspire my staff to be proud of what makes them different, as well as what makes them an important part of my business. My office is not just a place to work; it's a space for me and my team to be reminded of why we do what we do every single day—which is to sell beautiful products made by independent designers in the fashion, gift, and design world. It's *their* goals and dreams as small-business owners that motivate us as a company to bring beauty into the world along with an inviting and warm brand voice. In addition, we give back proceeds from every sale at MooreaSeal.com to nonprofits. There is meaning and motivation to help the world behind everything that we do. And it's these designers and people within nonprofits, most being women, that make me want to be a great business owner, a positive voice in social media, and the best version of myself that I can be.

Bringing this brand to life and finding self-confidence and pride in who I am as a creative woman definitely took a long time. Back in high school, I was deep into the arts, singing classical music almost forty hours a week in five separate choirs within and outside of school. I taught myself to play guitar at age fifteen and started writing my own music. I loved to paint and draw and write, but was I the best student in a traditional school setting? Nope. It was a mix of As, Cs, and Ds for me. I was driven in the arts but lacked comprehension and memory skills, and I struggled with depression, anxiety, and ADD from a young age. From age twelve until high school, I had big dreams of becoming a museum curator. But once I reached college, I quickly realized that despite intense studying, I just didn't have the capacity for memorization that the average person does, which is required to be an art history major. I'm great at making things and coming up with new ideas, but it's the retaining of information that proves difficult for me. As a result, I had to give up that dream and reroute to illustration, which to me felt like the perfect blend of two of my passions, creating art and storytelling. I dabbled in a few other majors including philosophy, apparel design, and studio art along the way as well.

Giving up my dream of becoming a museum curator was just a tiny part of what I've learned to let go of or put on hold as I've grown my career. At one point in 2010, I was a live-in nanny to a family of five, a nanny for another family forty hours a week, and an assistant to a sculptor, all while blogging seven to ten times a week, selling my own handmade jewelry on my Etsy shop (which was stocked in over forty stores worldwide), writing and performing my own music, and doing freelance graphic design and illustration for musicians and bloggers. Needless to say, I didn't really have a social life or any downtime. It was a *lot* to juggle and my "office" took many forms. When I was a live-in nanny, my bedroom barely fit a twin bed and a small Ikea desk. I shot all the photography for my Etsy shop on the dining room table and spent late nights designing, crafting, and packaging my jewelry at my desk or on my bed. I've had workstations in garages and basements, the worst one being a windowless, freezing garage that had no overhead light, one outlet, and demanded I wear up to five layers of clothes to stay warm! I've set up my home office in dining rooms and rented a small artist's studio. And the "office" where MooreaSeal.com was launched back in 2013 was in an old kids' playroom in a community center!

However, the one constant that I have kept with me in every "office" is a portrait of my grandmother. Because of all that she did over her lifetime during years when women were treated with far less respect than they are even today, I feel motivated to work as hard as I can in her honor. My grandmother's mom left my grandmother and her four siblings when she was a preteen, right at the time when she needed her mom most. But her half-Cherokee father (who endured more than you can imagine in the early 1900s) taught her that even in adversity, you can rise above with a strong will and compassion for yourself and for others. As she grew older, my grandmother channeled the pain of her youth into compassion for others struggling with trauma and hardships. She started the first three bilingual schools in the Los Angeles area and created the English as a Second Language program in 1975 that the national ESL program is now based on. During the Cold War, she also began an international student registration program to aid Cambodian communities in the greater Los Angeles area. Because of her example, I believe I can transform any traumas in my life into cultivating more compassion for others. That picture of her is the constant reminder that, through any hardship, there is always opportunity for change and progress!

I graduated college in 2009 with a degree in illustration, but because of the economic recession, I didn't see any traditional career opportunities open to me, so I was determined to create something for myself, nannying and working on a ton of creative businesses. My whole life I had identified as "Moorea who did everything" and I found a lot of self-worth in what I could *do* rather than who I *was* as a person. But no matter how much I did, I still felt lesser than my peers because of depression, anxiety, ADD, and my lack of comprehension and memorization skills, those things that ended my chances of being a museum curator. However, in late 2012, I noticed that my Pinterest following had grown to 250,000. I was beyond shocked and confused. Pinterest was the *one* space online that I was not working extremely hard to build out as part of my creative business. I was simply pinning what I loved and enjoying my time within that space—away from my other work. It was the first time that, despite being artistic my whole life and getting a degree in art, I could truly see my creative vision, my aesthetic, and my authentic personal style. I suddenly felt

like I was able to live a small portion of my dream of art curation through the world of social media. And when my Pinterest following grew to almost a million, I finally gave myself the chance to dream bigger about how I could *still* use my curatorial skills in a different way. It hit me that because I was being true to my own artistic vision, people were responding positively and engaging! I decided it was time to turn that skill into a new business—my online and physical store—while also recognizing that I needed to let go of a lot of things to achieve that new dream.

In 2013, I quit almost all of my many other career pursuits and artistic outlets (which were my bread and butter!) and took a huge risk with my cousin Reed and my friend Jenette to launch MooreaSeal.com. It was beyond terrifying letting go of all these creative paths to focus entirely on my retail site. I was afraid to lose my "Moorea who does everything" identity—and all the passions that came with it. But I learned something very valuable: Just because you are good at something doesn't mean that you *have* to do it. Just because you may have spent years investing in one path doesn't mean that it's the right one right now or that it's a reflection of your truest self. I didn't enjoy illustration or graphic design anymore, and my time spent on them was not only unprofitable but unfulfilling for my soul. The labels of designer, illustrator, musician, and nanny all felt more powerful than the actual experiences of living them daily.

So while it was incredibly scary, I trusted that though I needed to let go of many things to pursue one goal, it didn't mean that they would be lost forever. Now, just a few years later, I've seen many of them come back to me, like designing jewelry for my jewelry line, using graphic design and illustration to create my home goods line, and employing writing and art direction skills in the creation and design of my books.

My ability to adapt, grow, find new opportunities, help others through what I create, and make sound judgments are now the things I am most proud of—far more than my specific career achievements. Those are the things that make me feel connected to my grandmother even though she's no longer here with me. And those attributes are what I value most about my staff as well. We all have goals we are working toward together and, whether we achieve or fail, it's the pursuit and the passion that matters most and that inspires me and brings me fulfillment. In designing my office, I want that sentiment to seep into every crevice. That's why I love having tons of green plants (whether alive or fake) around to remind us that growth is more important than success or failure. Beautiful hanging baskets that I found at Ikea are stuffed with fake plants that I don't have to water to keep alive, but they still convey that message of growth in our space. The beautiful wood triangle shelf, built by our staff member Ashley, is to me a representation of what it means to lead by empowering others to thrive on their own through their unique skills. She had never used power tools before that shelf! She taught herself and made something amazing. The metal mobile of modern shapes from West Elm that hangs in a corner of the office reminds me of a giant piece of jewelry, the foundation upon which my business was built. Its unique design also reminds me of the originality of the designers' work featured in my store and, in a subtle way, keeps me searching for fresh, interesting, creative perspectives and new ideas to include in my brand as it grows.

At Home in Your Space

OFFICE

If there is any place in your home or at your job that should spark your creative juices, inspire new ideas, and make you feel empowered, it's your office. It really doesn't matter if you have a whole room to yourself, a cubicle, or just a collection of things in, say, your dining room cupboard that feel like guideposts to inspire your creative, personal, and professional pursuits. You can transform a corner with just a desk and a few affordable items that remind you of your dreams and goals. Maybe your personal motivators are colorful pens, pretty notebooks, uplifting quotes written down on paper, or objects made by people you admire—even your children's artwork or a photo of someone you look up to in your family! What matters most in styling your "office"— no matter its shape, size, or location—are the visuals to motivate you. You are the dictator of your dreams, so what can you decorate your office space with to remind you of the creativity, determination, and adaptability that are already living inside of you?

Consider your own space as you ponder these questions. Let your mind wander! Feel free to use the Notes section in the back of the book for journaling or sketching out ideas.

- What kind of work do you do? What kind of space do you need for that work?

- What are you most proud of accomplishing within the work realm?

- How does your work space spark creativity and productivity?

- What mood/vibe/feeling do you want your office to have?

- What colors reflect that mood?

- What decorative items do you already have that connect to that mood?

Being someone who loves art and décor but lacks a sharp memory, I love finding any way to create lists that remind me of who I am, what I love, and what motivates me. Collecting quotes from people who inspire me is a major way in which I get validation for who I am and what matters most to me. From jotting down inspiring quotes on paper to rotate in and out once a week on your home bulletin board depending on your mood, to painting and framing an inspiring quote to hang in your home year-round as a reminder of your chosen life's purpose, you can't go wrong with displaying quotes that mean a lot to you. Here are a few that I've carried with me throughout the years and have always kept me positive and inspired.

LET THE NIGHT BE TOO DARK FOR ME TO SEE. LET WHAT WILL BE, BE.

ROBERT FROST

TEN MOTIVATIONAL QUOTES

1 "Let the night be too dark for me to see. . . . Let what will be, be."
—ROBERT FROST

2 "It takes as much energy to wish as it does to plan."
—ELEANOR ROOSEVELT

3 "If you work really hard and are kind, amazing things will happen."
—CONAN O'BRIEN

4 "Nothing can dim the light which shines from within."
—MAYA ANGELOU

5 "To be yourself in a world that is constantly trying to make you
something else is the greatest accomplishment."
—RALPH WALDO EMERSON

6 "Life shrinks or expands in proportion to one's courage."
—ANAÏS NIN

7 "I have no special talent. I am only passionately curious."
—ALBERT EINSTEIN

8 "Don't ask what the world needs. Ask what makes you come alive,
and go do it. Because what the world needs is people who have
come alive." —HOWARD THURMAN

9 "Be soft. Do not let the world make you hard. Do not let pain make
you hate. Do not let the bitterness steal your sweetness. Take
pride that even though the rest of the world may disagree, you still
believe it to be a beautiful place." —IAIN S. THOMAS

10 "Failure meant a stripping away of the inessential."
—J. K. ROWLING

Make: IKEA DESK HACK

If you look closely at this book, you'll notice a lot of customizing and tweaking of furniture from affordable places like Ikea. We all live within our means and are down with style on a dime, so taking an affordable piece of furniture and adding something unique to it is a great way to create a one-of-a-kind vibe while living on a budget. I love how these legs give the desk a midcentury modern feel.

STEPS

1. Use painter's tape to mask off the metal bases on the bottom of the table legs so they don't get paint on them.

2. Sand the legs lightly with the 80- to 120-grit sandpaper. This is for smoothing and removing small imperfections.

3. Next sand with a 360- to 600-grit sandpaper. This is used to finish the surface smoothly.

4. Wipe down wood legs with a damp cloth to remove any debris.

5. Put on the gloves, and apply the stain with the sponge brush. Use just enough to saturate the wood (one dip with the tip of the sponge brush should suffice) and avoid dripping, as drips will appear in the stain once it's dried. Go with the grain to prevent streaks.

. . . continued

MATERIALS AND TOOLS

Painter's tape

4 (28-inch-long) midcentury modern–style table legs

1 sheet 80- to 120-grit sandpaper

1 sheet 360- to 600-grit sandpaper

Plastic gloves

Damp cloth

Brush or sponge brush (synthetic)

Water-based wood stain (I like the elegance of a dark walnut shade, but choose whatever tone you prefer)

Ikea tabletop (I used a white rectangular 59-by-29.5-inch "Linnmon" tabletop)

Measuring tape

Pencil

4 mounting plates, which come with screws

Drill or screwdriver

For information on where to buy materials and tools, see Resources (page 185).

6. Peel off the painter's tape from the metal bases and wipe off any stain that may have seeped through the tape with a damp cloth.

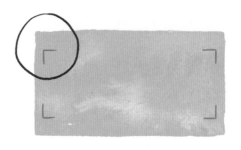

7. Let the stain dry for 6 to 8 hours (stand the tops of the legs on cardboard on the floor and lean the bottoms against a wall). Throw out your sponge brush.

8. Flip the tabletop upside down.

9. On one corner of the table bottom, measure 5 inches in from the longer side of the table edge and measure 2½ inches in from the shorter edge. This will create a right angle; pencil it in. This will be one of the corners where you align your mounting plate. Repeat on the other three corners. [see diagram]

9

10. Align the edge of one mounting plate with the right angle you drew. This is where your leg will attach. Repeat on all corners. (Ignore the predrilled holes on the bottom of the desk.) [see diagram]

10

11. Screw the mounts into the table bottom.

12. Attach the legs to the mounting plates by simply using your hands to screw the top of the leg into the hole in the center of the mounting plate. The angle of the legs should be jutting outward toward the long edge of the table.

13. Now flip the desk upright, take your cute new marbled mouse pad from the following page, and place it on top of your beautiful new desk for a refreshed and chic work space!

TIPS: When sanding always start with lower grits to remove dents and imperfections. Move up to the finer grits to achieve a clean and smooth finish.
   Wear plastic gloves when staining to avoid getting stain on your hands.

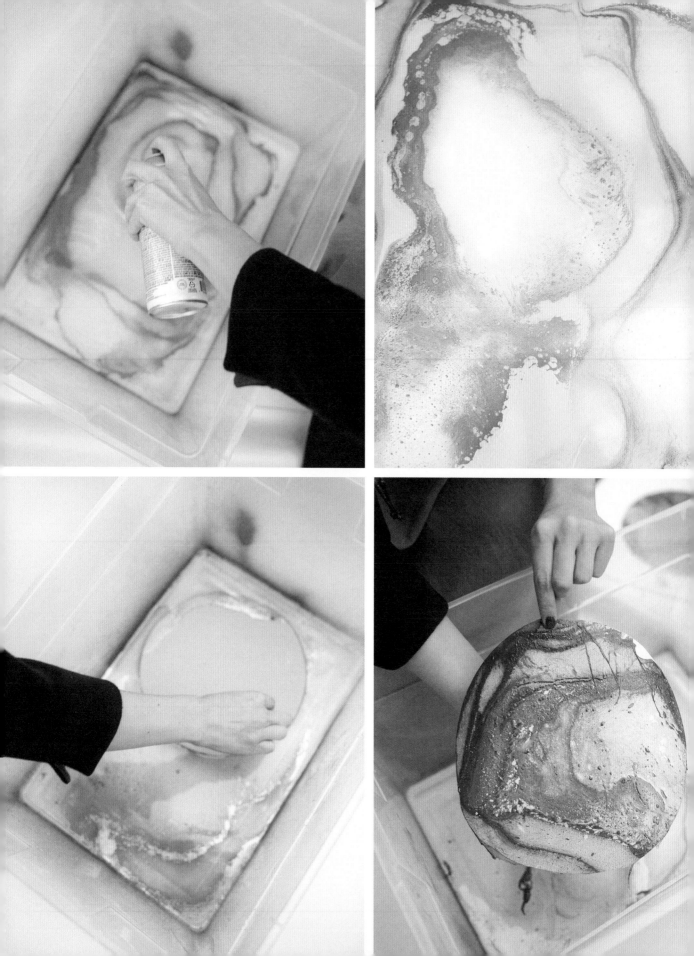

Make: MARBLED LEATHER MOUSE PAD

If you spend a significant amount of time at your computer, why settle for an ordinary mouse pad? Freshen up your desk with this unique luxe leather mouse pad with a metallic marbled design.

STEPS

1. Lay the leather piece upside down on a self-healing mat. Place the bowl on top of the leather and, using a marker, mark the shape of the circle on the leather. If you are able to cut the leather with scissors, cut out the circle shape. If it is too tough to cut with scissors, hold the bowl on the leather as an edge guide and use an X-Acto knife to cut out the shape.

2. Fill your plastic tub with 2 to 3 inches of water.

3. Spray your two spray-paint colors directly into the water to create a marbled effect. The movement of the water creates swirls of spray-paint color. Use a toothpick to swirl the colors around more if you want more movement in your marbled design to transfer to the leather.

4. Now gently place the leather top side down into the tub and pull back up as soon as possible. The marbled spray paint will transfer as soon as it touches the leather!

5. Repeat this as many times as needed to cover the entire surface of the leather in marbled paint. The spray paint may be a bit lumpy in some spots at first, but once you let it dry, you can press those areas down with a heavy book and they will lie flat.

6. Let dry for 3 hours. Then add it to your desktop and start working in style!

MATERIALS AND TOOLS

1 (12-by-12-inch) piece thick leather, faux leather (avoid leather with a lot of texture or any embossing; smooth leather tends to work better here), or upholstery vinyl

Self-healing mat

Large bowl the same size you want your mouse pad to be (smaller than 12 inches in diameter)

Marker

X-Acto knife or scissors

Plastic tub (wide enough to fit your cut piece of leather)

Water

2 spray paint colors (I used navy blue and copper)

Toothpick

For information on where to buy materials and tools, see Resources (page 185).

TIP: Here in Seattle, we have a wonderful leather store called MacPherson Leather Company that has both an online retail site and a storefront. In the store, they have a bin of scrap leather, which is where I like to get my leathers. And it's usually at a super-discounted price. Waste not, want not! See if there are any local leather companies in your area and call them to check if they have discounted scrap leather. Or ask if your local fabric store carries leather as well.

Kim Kogane

English, she came back to Alaska in the middle of a recession and couldn't find a job. So she took a risk and moved to Portland, Oregon. After finding a day job at a call center, Kim knew straight away that it was a bad fit. She sat down at a coffee shop and made a list of her skills, quickly realizing a new dream of being her own boss and designing jewelry. In her spare time after work, she began making jewelry, selling it at craft fairs, and stocking her jewelry line in stores. Then just one year after living in Portland, she risked leaving her day job and ventured out on her own with her jewelry business. "I was working from home to save money . . . me on this couch," she says, pointing out the green velvet, jewel-toned vintage sofa that is a focal point of her inspiring office/studio and visual reminder of where she's been.

WHAT SHE'S KNOWN FOR: Her stacking rings, a collection of tiny gold and silver bands with varying thicknesses, textures, and patterns. At my store, they're one of our best sellers!

WHAT SHE LOVES: Delicate, detailed patterns; lush textures; natural wood; antiques; pops of pink and dark green; simplicity; subtle details, like when you look at something and feel like you've discovered a secret treasure. Her studio has so many quiet moments that evoke that feeling, from touches of velvet against clean marble to her collection of ornate brass animal figurines.

WHERE SHE FINDS INSPIRATION: Traveling and seeing unique landscapes, colors, and textures around the globe excite her. To gain inspiration at home, her walks around her studio's Pioneer Square neighborhood, which, with its brick buildings and rich local history, reminds her of mini New York or Paris.

KIM KOGANE

Jewelry designer/owner of Fresh Tangerine

LIVES IN: Seattle, Washington

FROM: Anchorage, Alaska

SIGNATURE STYLE: functional minimalism meets feminine bohemian

HOW SHE BECAME A JEWELRY DESIGNER AND SMALL BUSINESS OWNER: Making jewelry had always been a hobby for Kim. She planned to become an architect, but after graduating college and spending a year in France teaching

I was lucky to meet Kim a few years ago at a pop-up shop where I was selling goods from my store. After getting to know her and checking out her jewelry line, I not only knew that I had to stock her minimal and chic rings and necklaces at my own store, but also knew we would become fast friends. We have so much in common, in how we turned a jewelry-making hobby into a thriving business during the recession but also in the way our personal lives and childhoods have deeply influenced our career paths and our personal philosophies. At a young age, we both took on a lot of responsibilities within our families—which at the time was not ideal. We grew up fast and, in doing so, found strength and purpose via the lofty goals we set for ourselves. As adults, we have both found confidence and pride in what we know we can achieve because, through challenging experiences, we cultivated similar skills that we use to improve our lives and the lives of others—through hard work and dedication to our dreams. It's an honor to have a friend like Kim in the world of fashion and small business. Kim's wholesale jewelry business and retail shop in Seattle's historic Pioneer Square neighborhood sells to over forty boutiques nationwide and in Canada, including the Moorea Seal store. She's a true reflection of what it means to be a woman in business, which takes incredible determination, a willingness to keep going in the face of adversity, self-reliance, and trust in one's intuition. We also both believe in empowering other women through our work, setting examples just as we did as big sisters for our little sisters. I hope you find Kim—and her beautiful office—as inspiring as I do.

KIM'S OFFICE/STUDIO

On a corner of Pioneer Square, Fresh Tangerine is hidden inside an old brick building next to a hip saloon, just steps away from the Puget Sound waterfront. The sun-drenched, airy, loftlike space with huge door-sized windows looks out onto the hustle and bustle of the neighborhood. Though there are no walls separating the showroom from the work space, Kim has managed to make clear divisions within, while not sacrificing a harmonious flow. Antiques and old pieces are cleverly juxtaposed against Ikea shelves and tables and girlie pops, like bright-pink chairs and gold heart decals on a wall. Since her jewelry is mostly gold and features clean lines and simple geometric shapes (with some precious stones incorporated here and there), it was important to her to convey that understated

richness in her office space as well.

To give her customers a place to feel comfy while playing around with the jewelry, she's created a sitting room that feels a lot like someone's lovely living area. Besides the amazing green couch, there's also a gold Moroccan-style pouf, brightly colored, printed woolen rugs layered over each other, midcentury modern white chairs draped with fur, and two shapely white coffee tables with an antique pink perfume atomizer, green plants, and jewelry boxes on top. But while that overt femininity is present, Kim's space is also where she works, literally, both designing jewelry and dealing with the day-to-day tasks of being a business owner and boss. So on the other side of the room, it's much more stark, with an organizing principle that resists clutter. Her jewelry-making tools hang neatly on the walls and a big white dining-size table allows her and her employees to gather for meetings or work on jewelry.

HOW KIM'S OFFICE REFLECTS HER AESTHETIC AND WORKING STYLE

"I knew I had all this space, so I could create a physical place where people who like the brand can come to if they're in Seattle. That's how the whole showroom space came about. I'm a very visual person and hugely affected by the space I'm in. I'm all about function and comfort, so I wanted something inspiring but also comfortable, where I could come in and feel like I'm at home. Being an entrepreneur, so much of your work is very unstable, you have to go with the flow and change on a whim. I cope with that by making my space feel very cozy and homey so I'm able to be comfortable in business." It's especially important to her that her space provides the opportunity for movement. "I like a lot of change throughout my day, so I'll be at my bare-bones desk on the computer if I'm really focusing, but if I'm writing a blog post, I'm on the couch surrounded by color and textures. If I want to be around people, I sit at the big table with my team." If you take anything away from Kim's story—even if your office is probably not a business open to the public with a showroom—it should be the idea of creating a space that allows for a change in your state of mind or work pace as your day unfolds. To give herself inspiration while she's working at the computer, she looks to a simple bulletin board on the wall next to her, where she pins things she cuts out from magazines or anything she sees that brings her artistic vibes, even if it's just a color sample. That's something simple that anyone can do, regardless of how big or small their space. Or maybe, like Kim, you have room for a stand-out couch or love seat, a fashionable rug, or a collection of quirky objects that's a respite from your orderly desk.

She says that Fresh Tangerine is a combination of the girlie part of her personality mixed with her subtler, natural style. And because it's so important to her to keep her jewelry affordable, she wants her space to feel equally approachable, which is why she cleaves to a budget, finding sneaky ways to repurpose Ikea furniture, for example, which is something anyone can do, regardless of how big or small their space. "I kind of like having those limitations. I use the Ikea pieces as a foundation and want them to blend with the existing space, but [I] don't expect to get the design details from there. That's where you go vintage and handmade, like with art from Etsy or through trades with other artists at craft fairs."

"Society tells women that certain things are important: you have to be likable, please everyone, share your ideas, but you don't want them to be too big, to take up too much space. I want to say: it's OK to be proud of what you've accomplished and take a stand for yourself."

KIM'S TIPS
for Being a Leader in Your Life

Besides selling beautiful jewelry, Kim is also passionate about helping other young women who want to run their own businesses, and she works hard to cultivate a work environment that is supportive while also taking charge. And whether you're a boss or simply trying to assert yourself at home or in your community, her tips cross over. "Society tells women that certain things are important: you have to be likable, please everyone, share your ideas, but you don't want them to be too big, to take up too much space. I want to say: It's OK to be proud of what you've accomplished and take a stand for yourself. Your opinions are valid and it's OK to say them, and it's OK to make people mad. Not everyone has to like your opinion."

- If you're afraid to state your opinion or you're scared someone won't like it, try to do it anyway to set an example of bravery.

- Sometimes you have to disappoint one person for the greater good. That's OK; trust your intuition.

- You can be a leader and still be kind. Build people up; it creates more success for everyone.

- Listen to other people's input, especially the people you trust and the people you lead.

- There's no one-size-fits-all approach to being a leader. You can be assertive and in charge, but it's OK to stay true to yourself at the same time. If you're more laid-back, that can come through in your leadership style.

Bedroom

Creating a Private Sanctuary

IF THERE'S ANY ROOM IN A HOME that reflects your most genuine, vulnerable self, it has to be the bedroom. It's our own personal sanctuary, the space most deeply connected to personal wellness and self-care—rest, relaxation, and self-expression in particular. When we were kids, self-care and self-expression in a bedroom had a lot to do with how we tacked up posters of bands we loved and drawings we made, strewing our clothes all over the floor and jumping on the bed. For adults, it typically manifests through soaking up sleep, spending time with someone you love, retreating into your own quiet space, or choosing clothes that define your personality. Whether you're a single person who enjoys total self-expression in your bedroom or someone who shares the bedroom with a roommate or a partner, the comfort, peace, and freedom there are paramount to your daily well-being. Ask any mom or dad; a few minutes of quiet spent in the bedroom with no kids knocking at the door is a moment in heaven. And for those without children, like me, it's an intimate space where we can be exactly who we want to be, free from society's judgement.

I'm someone who needs a lot of alone time to recharge. I'm super friendly and love meeting new people, but my energy is drained when I'm around others for too long, and the only way I regain it is through time spent in quiet. I'm a mega introvert. I'm also not the best at following through with self-care, which is a major reason why I wrote the 52 Lists journal series as an exercise in self-help for myself. I crave visual reminders of what I need and want for my personal wellness, what motivates me and inspires me in investing not only in my health, but in my identity. So designing a bedroom that fully reflects the calm I want to feel on the inside and the creativity and quirk that are true to my personality—and my husband's—is very important to me. My business demands a lot from me. I usually work at least ten to twelve hours a day and spend a few hours working every weekend, so I savor the retreat back into my bedroom each night with my husband and my dog like it's a sacred treasure.

The dark gray/blue wall beside our bed sets the calm and contemplative mood for the room. My husband and I are very private and gentle spirited. But under our mellow surfaces, we are also quite complex, and our favorite moments together are during deep conversations about what really matters to us in life. We are thinkers and feelers, and the deep shade is a true reflection of our energy together, quiet at times but passionate and strong as well. Since the darker wall is so dominant, I've decorated it with pieces that add texture and lightness: my North Star Mirror (page 117), a rattan mirror from Target, an illustrated print of antlers by my friend and designer Jessica Rose from VOL25, and a bull skull that once belonged to my dad, bringing more complexity to our space and illustrating the balance of our personalities.

Throughout our room, I've also created little vignettes that embody unique elements of our identities. Though we don't feel comfortable living with society's prescribed gender roles of men not being allowed to express emotion or women being deemed unfeminine if they are strong willed, there are still times when we fall into a balance, a yin and yang of feminine and masculine energy. For couples of any gender, bedrooms are obviously a space of intimacy, emotionally and physically. Having the room, privacy, and feeling of safety to explore the feminine and masculine sides of self is so important and sacred. And in styling our bedroom, I want to reflect that balance in our shared space while also allowing room for us to be individuals. Just take a look at our respective dressers and you'll get an idea of how each of our personalities emerge.

My favorite part of my bedroom is hands down my gorgeous antique dresser—one that I had in my bedroom growing up. It feels like a one-of-a-kind piece, with its unique wood grain and beautiful curving shapes. My enthusiasm about the rare, mysterious, and treasured isn't represented by just the outside of my dresser but also the inside where more treasures are found: the beautiful things that I use to style myself and find joy in the freedom of self-adornment. I recognize that it may be more instinctual for most people to view the bathroom as a place of private self-care, and hell yes, I love a good bubble bath to unwind and center myself. But for me, that self-care—the love and respect of my identity, my body, and my ability to be innovative and enthusiastic about what is new and what can be reworked again—is all found within the treasure box of my dresser and little closet.

Not only is dressing a huge part of my identity because of my business and brand within the fashion world; it's also a daily practice and ritual that we all participate in whether we think about it or not. Each day, we choose how to present ourselves to the world through the costume we put on, be it relaxed with a T-shirt and jeans, professional and serious with a clean and tailored outfit,

free-spirited with a long-flowing and patterned maxi dress, or something totally outside the norm that shows off a provocative and interesting side of ourselves. How we care for our body starts in the kitchen with the nourishment of food and the bathroom through cleaning ourselves up. But how we style or intentionally *don't style* ourselves after all our other self-care routines are done is the final and key piece in loving ourselves well—at least for me—even though it is often overlooked or deemed superficial.

When I'm battling anxiety and depression daily, waking up to beauty and taking the time to clothe myself in pieces I love really helps start things off positively. Some days I feel super intimidated to wear something that feels a little more daring or bold with wild patterns and color. Getting dressed can be a challenge when you let the outside world's voices infiltrate your own perspective. Even close friends' opinions can make me nervous. I vividly recall a time when a guy in my friend group in college cornered me to ask: "Why do you dress so differently from all of our friends? You look like you're trying too hard, you're superficial, and all you care about are clothes." He's not a friend anymore, obviously. Friends don't judge you based on how you look. As a thirtysomething woman, I can look back on that and think, *Well, that was pretty crappy!*—he was a little bit like a bully from an eighties teen flick. But even though those comments hold no validity, moments like those from the past still make me worry about the negative feedback I could get as a grown woman just trying to have fun with clothes and style.

A few years ago, I actively posted photos of my outfits on my blog, and I made the bad choice of reading pages and pages of hateful comments from anonymous strangers ripping me apart for what I wear and how I look. Since then, I haven't allowed myself to go back and reread them, but I still feel a tinge of anxiety when I post almost anything on my blog, my Instagram account, or wherever I share my true and honest perspective. But it doesn't stop me. For every piece of online hate, there's a person out there who I might help get out of a rut, inspire, or simply make smile by being authentic to myself. And in doing so, I hope I can inspire others to find courage to do the same. That, above all else, is my greatest goal in all that I do.

Even with other people's judgment nagging at the back of my mind, I pursue celebrating myself through what I wear and through my investment in self-care. When I feel good about myself and find certainty in my heart, my mind, and my intentions, it's easier to trust that I'm not dressing to impress my peers, my friends, or even my husband. And when I focus less on what society says my body needs to look like and let my worries about what people will say about how I dress fade away, the celebration of playing with patterns that inspire me, colors that bring me happiness, and silhouettes that are interesting to experiment with fills my soul with confidence in *me*. That is *really* what waking up is all about—choosing to trust in your unique perspective each morning, day after day. Taking time to enjoy the space of my bedroom and relish the process of playing with clothes and accessories is the visual reminder that I have chosen to invest in myself!

At Home in Your Space

BEDROOM

Think about how you inhabit your most private space and what you do to cultivate a sense of self-care there. Like it is for me, it might be a place that fulfills a few aspects of loving yourself well, from the enjoyment of styling yourself every morning or journaling to start your day off with a clear mind, to the end-of-the-day ritual of kicking off your shoes, getting into your favorite pajamas, and snuggling up with someone you love (including cute pets) to watch a movie with a calming candle burning nearby. Whatever the things that bring you comfort, confidence, and peace, keep investing in them within your bedroom. This is your most intimate space. Let the way you decorate it be a reflection of how you care for and love *you*.

Consider your own space as you ponder these questions. Let your mind wander! Feel free to use the Notes section in the back of the book for journaling or sketching out ideas.

- How do you like to take care of yourself?

- What brings you rest and calm?

- What did you love about your bedroom as a child?

- What mood/vibe/feeling do you want your bedroom to have?

- What colors reflect that mood?

- What decorative items do you already have that connect to that mood?

- What sorts of scents/candles do you like to have in this space?

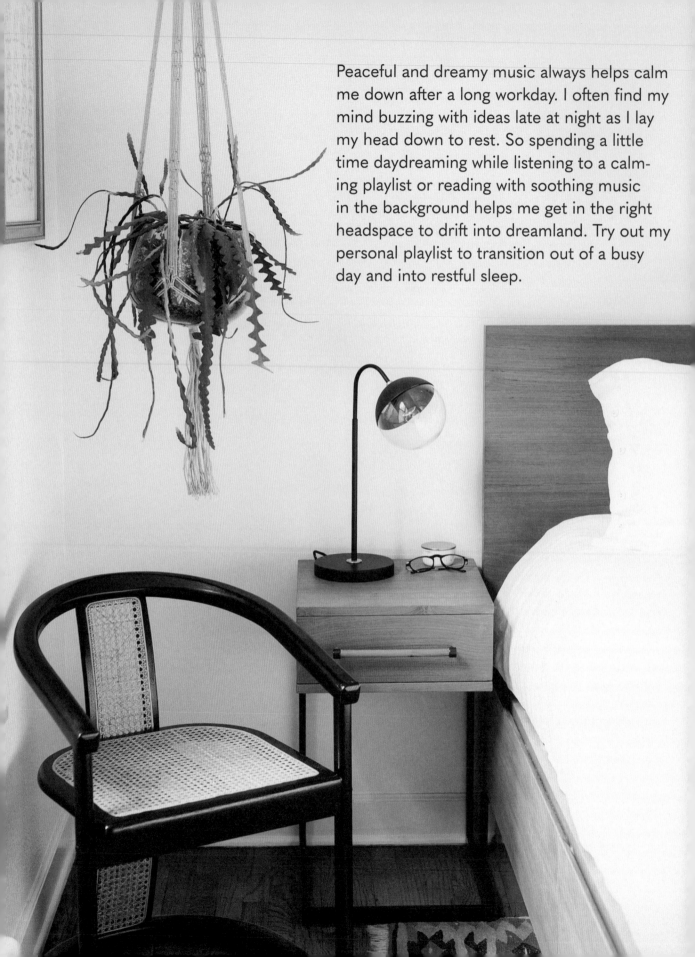

Peaceful and dreamy music always helps calm me down after a long workday. I often find my mind buzzing with ideas late at night as I lay my head down to rest. So spending a little time daydreaming while listening to a calming playlist or reading with soothing music in the background helps me get in the right headspace to drift into dreamland. Try out my personal playlist to transition out of a busy day and into restful sleep.

DEEP SLEEP PLAYLIST

1 "Harvest Moon" —NEIL YOUNG

2 "Mirrorball" —ELBOW

3 "On & On" —ERYKAH BADU

4 "Nothin' in the World Can Stop Me Worryin'
'Bout That Girl" —THE KINKS

5 "Heartbeats" —JOSÉ GONZÁLEZ

6 "I See Monsters" —RYAN ADAMS

7 "Magnetized" —LAURA VEIRS

8 "Helplessly Hoping" —CROSBY, STILLS & NASH

9 "Pink Moon" —NICK DRAKE

10 "Good Night" —THE BEATLES

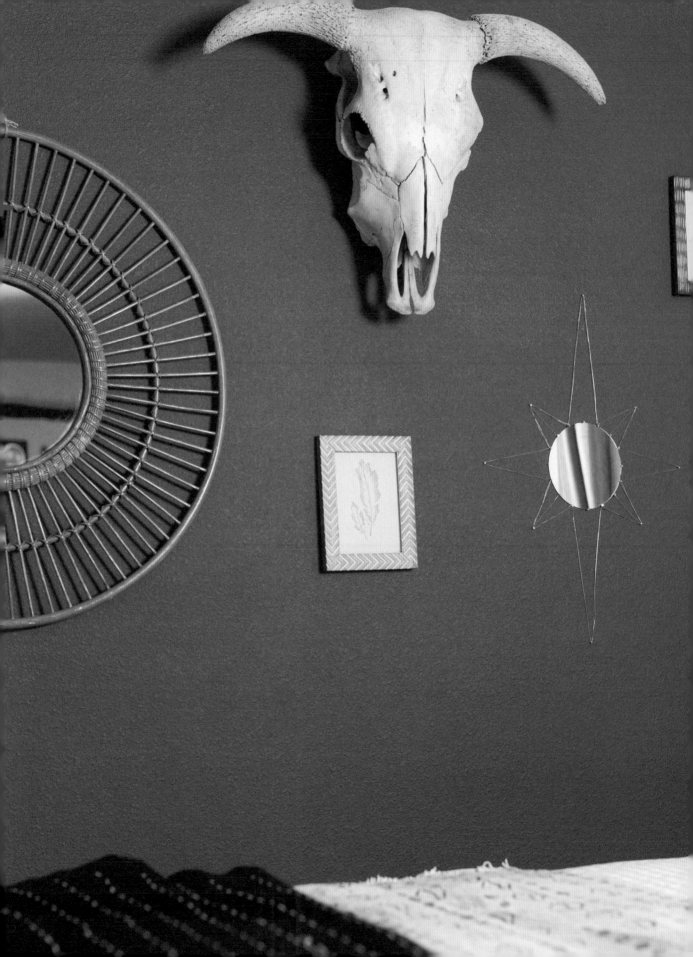

Make: NORTH STAR MIRROR

Whether the sun is shining outdoors or the rain is coming down, this North Star mirror adds a dash of radiant celestial shine to your bedroom, morning and night. Just make sure to choose the location of your mirror carefully—you'll be nailing holes into your wall, so this is a permanent piece of décor. If you don't want to commit to a permanent location, you could also do this on a piece of wood and then hang that up on your wall or lean it against a wall on top of your dresser.

STEPS

1. Place the mirror on the wall where you want to hang it, using your hand to hold it in place. Make sure to leave space to build the star's rays. [see diagram on the following page]

2. Hammer four nails around the edge of the mirror, at twelve, three, six, and nine o'clock. The mirror should sit tightly underneath the head of the nails. (The nails are holding the mirror in place.) [see diagram on the following page]

3. Hammer in four more nails, evenly spaced between the first four nails. These should not be hammered in fully (about halfway in), as wire will be wrapped around them. Now hammer in eight more nails about halfway in, evenly spaced between the existing nails, for a total of sixteen nails (twelve of them should be raised). [see diagram on the following page]

4. After the nails are secure, label each nail with a piece of tape with a number written on it, starting with number 1 at twelve o'clock and working your way around the nails clockwise. [see diagram on the following page]

. . . continued

MATERIALS AND TOOLS

6-inch frameless round glass mirror

24 (½-inch- to 1-inch-long) brass nails

30 feet of 24-gauge dead-soft brass wire ("dead soft" means the wire hasn't been hardened and is still easy to bend), precut into:

2 (40-inch) large star points

2 (26-inch) medium star points

4 (16-inch) mini star points

4 (7-inch) smallest pieces

Wire cutters

Hammer

Masking tape

Pencil

For information on where to buy materials and tools, see Resources (page 185).

40 in

26 in

16 in

7 in

5. Measure 9 inches directly down from nail 9 and mark on the wall with a pencil as nail 19. Measure 9 inches directly up from nail 1 and mark on the wall with a pencil as nail 17. Hammer in nails at those spots, halfway in. Measure out 5 inches from nail 5 and mark with a pencil as nail 18. Measure out 5 inches from nail 13 and mark as nail 20. Hammer in nails at these spots, halfway in. [see diagram]

6. Gather the two 40-inch wires. Starting at nail 10, wrap one end of one wire around the whole nail tightly about four times, then pull it down and wrap it around nail 19 two times. From there, bring it up to nail 8 and wrap it around twice; bring the wire back down to nail 19 and then back up to nail 10, where you started. Wrap the end around nail 10 four times again and then cut off any extra. This is your first ray. [see diagram]

7. Repeat this method of wrapping and tying off with the second piece of 40-inch wire, starting with nail 16, going up to nail 17, down to nail 2, back to 17, and then back to nail 16.

8. Repeat this same wrapping method with the two 26-inch-long wires for the two side star nail groups: 12, 20, and 14; 4, 18, and 6.

9. Now that you have your outer star points, you can move on to the four inner points. Measure out 3 inches from nails 15, 3, 7, and 11 and mark on the wall with pencil where you will be placing your next grouping of nails. Starting with the upper-left-hand nail, number each nail, going clockwise, 21, 22, 23, and 24. [see diagram]

10. Hammer in nails at those spots, halfway in. Using the four 16-inch pieces of wire, continue the method of wrapping and tying off for the following groups of nails: 14, 21 and 16; 2, 22, and 4; 6, 23, and 8; 10, 24, and 9. [see diagram]

11. For the last detail, using the four 7-inch wires, wrap one wire each between 15 and 21, 3 and 22, 7 and 23, and 11 and 24. [see diagram]

12. Using your wire cutters, cut off any excess wire that may be left over on any of the star points. Do not double back with any extra wire that you may have.

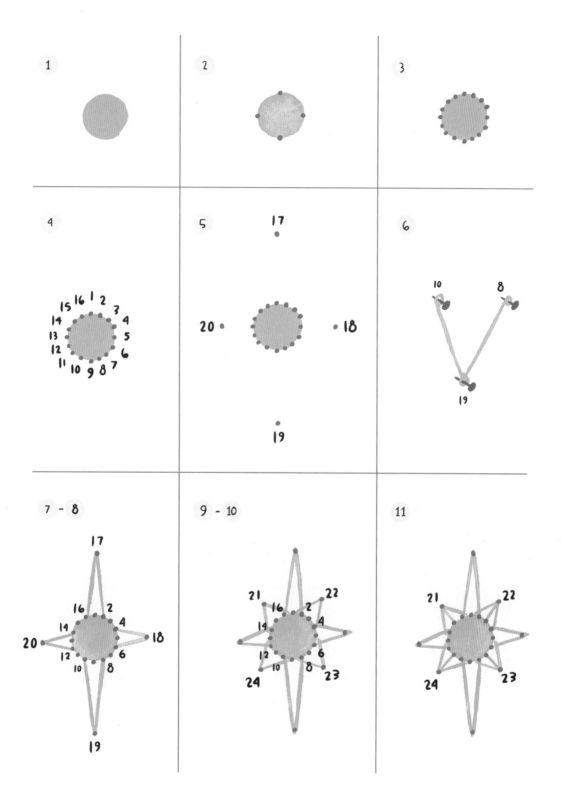

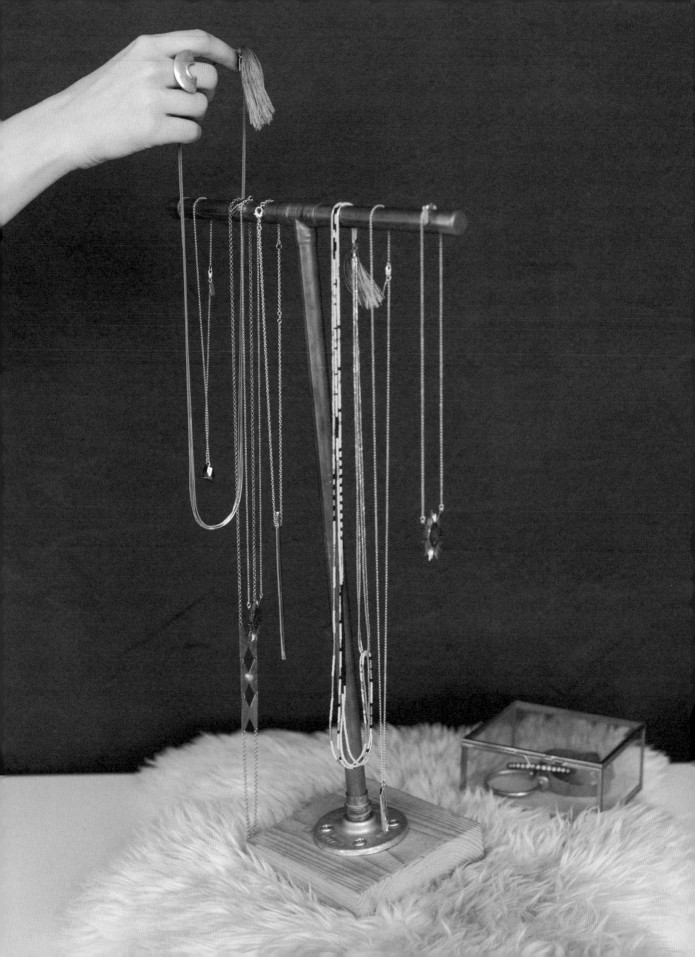

Make: COPPER PIPE NECKLACE DISPLAY

You can probably guess that I have quite a bit of jewelry since I own a retail store focused on accessories! These copper pipe jewelry displays offer a rustic and unique way to display your jewelry atop a dresser or shelf. I created these for my store's jewelry displays and sometimes switch out hanging my necklaces on antlers on my wall for hanging them on this copper pipe display.

STEPS

1. Push the two 6-inch copper pipes into two opposing ends of the pressure tee, then place the end caps on the two arms.

2. Push the 18-inch copper pipe into the remaining hole in the pressure tee, then push the opposite end into the pressure adapter (the base of the display).

3. Once you have decided that it looks good, try to take everything apart. If it comes apart easily, you can super-glue inside each end cap and pressure tee to solidify the frame in place. Or, if they all stick in place pretty well, you don't have to glue any of the parts at all!

4. Sand the wood block with the 80- to 120-grit sandpaper to get rid of any really rough edges and surfaces. Next sand with 360- to 600-grit sandpaper to get it nice and soft and smooth.

5. Screw the floor flange into the center of the wood block using the wood screws.

6. Screw the base of the copper jewelry display, the adapter, into the floor flange. You now have yourself a beautiful, rustic spot to hang all of your favorite necklaces!

. . . continued

MATERIALS AND TOOLS

2 (6-inch) pieces ½-inch copper pipe (have your pipe cut at a local hardware store)

1 (½-inch) copper pressure tee

2 (½-inch) copper end caps

1 (18-inch) piece ½-inch copper pipe

1 (½-inch) copper pressure C x MIP adapter (sometimes known as a male adapter)

Superglue (optional)

Wood block (I had the folks at Home Depot cut down the end of a two-by-four into a 2-by-4-by-4-inch block)

1 sheet 80- to 120-grit sandpaper

1 sheet 360- to 600-grit sandpaper

4 short wood screws

1 (½-inch) iron floor flange

Drill or screwdriver

For information on where to buy materials and tools, see Resources (page 185).

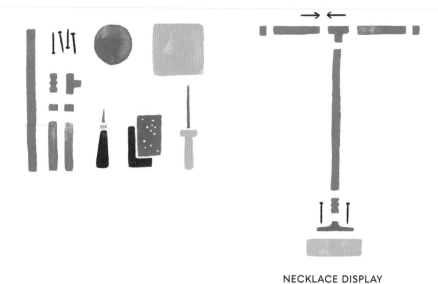

NECKLACE DISPLAY

VARIATION: BRACELET DISPLAY

To make a bracelet display, follow the instructions on the previous page, simply replacing the 18-inch pipe with another 6-inch pipe.

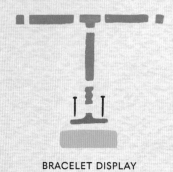

BRACELET DISPLAY

VINTAGE VIBES WITH
Erin Perez Hagstrom

ERIN PEREZ HAGSTROM

Freelance writer and blogger at
CaliVintage, *and formerly at ModCloth*

LIVES IN: Redlands, California

FROM: Redlands, California

SIGNATURE STYLE: celebrating vintage and handmade through adaptable design

HOW SHE BECAME A BLOGGER: Erin didn't set out to become a fashion blogger. When she was growing up in Redlands, her first job in high school was at a vintage shop and record store, working in the back room picking through truck-loads of stuff and deciding what to sell on eBay—from Zippo lighters to vintage Levi's that sold for hundreds of dollars in Japan where American vintage goods were highly coveted. "That was my education, what definitely led me to where I am now," she says. "This was before all the vintage sellers started coming up. I was just sitting there doing listings." From there, she began her ultra popular, fashion-focused blog *CaliVintage* and was eventually noticed by Susan Koger, the founder of ModCloth, who invited her to come work for them in the San Francisco office. It was an offer she couldn't pass up. Years later, though, after she and her partner had soaked up all that the city had to offer, they found their way back to her hometown to invest in the community where Erin's life journey first began and to raise their growing family. Her blog, *CaliVintage*, is still alive and well after all these years and is growing along with her—no longer focused only on fashion, it now highlights her new love of home décor and her devotion to thoughtful living and family as well.

WHAT SHE LOVES: vintage, vintage, vintage—from clothes to home décor, simplicity and uncluttered spaces, neutral and subtly warm tones, midcentury modern and antique, small doses of seventies retro décor, slow living and slowly decorating over time, unique art objects, Japanese minimalism, Montessori-inspired design, woven baskets, plants

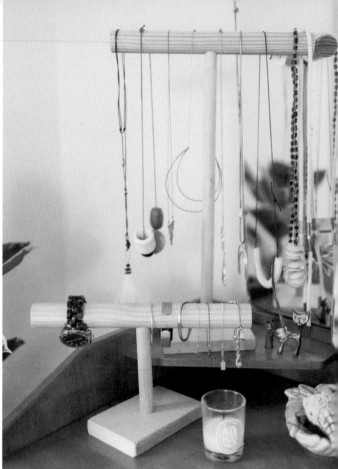

I've always admired Erin's dedication to mindful living, valuing the investments she makes in clothing, home décor, her community, and so much more. She believes in doing things with intention, and she gives herself time and space to really think carefully about what matters most to her in how she lives her life and how she styles her space. I also related to Erin's journey of growing up and wanting to escape the confines of a small town to discover what she was passionate about within a big city with a million opportunities and perspectives. As we have both grown older and worked really hard at creating careers for ourselves that give us full creative control, we've both realized what matters to us most beyond money or any career accomplishment we can achieve: letting our hearts and our truest intentions guide us. To me, Erin illustrates

the life that I hope to cultivate: a peaceful and loving emotional state and an equally inviting and calming space within my home. You can easily and quickly fill a house with pretty objects and trendy décor to reflect what the outside world says is "perfect." But it's the love and the thoughtfulness behind the stuff that make objects meaningful, more valuable than their monetary value. And this is the life that Erin so beautifully illustrates as she lives day to day with her adorable family in a space that fulfills their needs and reflects their genuine nature.

WHAT'S OLD IS NEW AGAIN

Erin never imagined she'd end up in her small hometown of Redlands, California, again, but when she and her partner decided they wanted

to have children, suddenly the small-town life and the proximity of her large Mexican and Native American family made Redlands seem more ideal than San Francisco. "When I was growing up in Redlands, I was like, 'I hate this place, I hate suburbia, I'm never moving back.' Then . . . things change. I didn't realize that it's a really nice place to raise a family; it's actually incredibly charming with a lot of vintage homes and historic landmarks. Maybe that's why I love vintage houses so much. I have deep roots in this area." Of course, given her love of vintage, she knew she needed to find a very specific type of home. "I didn't even look at houses that weren't vintage or in the historic district. I wanted to be a part of

"If you find something vintage, it's something that survived all this time, because it was built well and because it has a timeless quality to it."

this community. I knew that I wanted a cool vintage house that hadn't been flipped. I knew it would need work, but I wanted to restore it. It's a piece of history that's been here since the 1920s. I can't stand to see, especially nowadays, how real estate has changed. Companies gut it, ruin it, and sell it for a profit to someone who can afford it. My plan isn't that one day we're going to fix this up and then sell it and get a bigger house. That's not what I'm looking for. This is the life I want to live."

Her house has only been renovated once, in 1970, and the owners did some wacky stuff like plastering over doors, installing an avocado-green kitchen and sickly sea-foam-green tiles, and covering the original hardwood floors in green shag. "But there is a lot that is original in this house. Back in that time, things were built and created thoughtfully. The wood floors are like an inch thick; they don't do that anymore. So that's what I appreciate. If you find something vintage, it's something that survived all this time, because it was built well and because it has a timeless quality to it. It's something that didn't go out of fashion. Even if I buy something new, it's the same concept: it could have been made in the fifties or the twenties, it's something that's going to survive, it's meaningful. When it comes to décor, the house is 1920s but I'm not trying to be only period literal." Instead, she cleaves to the architecture of the house in terms of fixtures—from brass switch plates to push-button light switches—while bringing in midcentury modern and seventies accents to the décor. "This house is not perfect. But I sit and daydream about it. It's good to dream and think about what it could be, to plan, to look ahead."

INTENTIONAL LIVING

Erin's commitment to quality and timelessness informs not just her style but also how she raises her family. With a toddler son and a baby daughter, Erin has had to adapt her house to their needs while she also juggles her work-from-home lifestyle. That's why her bedroom is in constant flux—a place where she does everything from nursing to blogging. It's also why she's attracted to progressive parenting philosophies, like the Montessori method, which she incorporates into her home. The underlying ethos is that children need to learn life skills and independence, and giving them the tools to do that is of utmost importance.

That's why you'll see pretty baskets around the house (where her son Adam can find various activities) as well as a bed on the floor that he can climb in and out of without any help, a kid-level coat rack so he can dress himself, and a gender-neutral, serene bedroom filled with plants and natural wood that doesn't overstimulate. "He loves trucks, that's cool, but I'm not going to buy him a bunch of trucks and T-shirts with trucks. I don't want to pigeonhole him into one thing just because he was into it for two weeks. Also, I don't like that culture of 'throw everything away,' throw-away toys that are crappy and break in ten minutes." She feels the same about all the pieces she buys, including furniture. She tries to buy things that she'll be able to use anywhere in the house, like her standing desk and a rocking chair sometimes used in the living room and currently in the kids' bedroom. "Anything that happens in my life is because I'm incredibly flexible. I'm very open and receptive to whatever is coming my way at any moment. And that's how I do my house too. If you visit, it's changing all the time. It's this living, breathing space that I adapt to the life of my son and daughter, my whole family."

HOW ERIN'S BEDROOM REFLECTS HER LIFE

You'd never know by looking at her minimalist but pretty bedroom that Erin never decorated a bedroom before in her entire adult life. "It was always just dump stuff in . . . massive piles of laundry and a bed. But it feels really good to have a serene space." While a huge bed takes up a large part of the room—it's big enough so that both of her kids can pile in with them—it also has a Moses basket that she found a vintage stand for, perfect for when the baby is sleeping and she needs to work (it's

transportable from room to room), plants, baskets for laundry, affirming artwork on the white walls, and her very special midcentury vanity—the one piece of the bedroom that is truly hers, and the most important way that she invests in herself while juggling the demands of motherhood and work. "I always wanted a vanity, always wanted to sit and put on my makeup. It's such a glamorous idea. It's such a small thing in a way but makes a huge difference. It's so cool to have a huge vanity with all my makeup, lotions, and jewelry, and it feels really feminine and frivolous in a good way." Plus, it's actually necessary to her well-being as a work-at-home mom: getting ready every morning makes her feel "human and alive" and more productive, even if she doesn't see anyone besides her kids or her partner that day. Of course, true to her parenting style, she also lets her son play with her brushes and bottles and nail polish. "He'll come and hang out with me and watch me do my thing. It's cute because he shares that experience with me."

ERIN'S TIPS

for Buying Pieces to Last a Lifetime

There is something so special about having vintage pieces in your home. Not only does finding a vintage treasure offer you the opportunity to highlight a truly unique piece of furniture that none of your friends have, but it also gives you the chance to discover which past decades resonate most deeply with you. There is also a sustainability element to choosing something vintage over a new piece of furniture or something mass produced that will most likely break in five to ten years and will be thrown in a landfill. By choosing vintage, you're protecting the planet, one little decorating choice at a time. Investing in vintage furniture will also save you money over time as the value of something vintage only increases (you can resell it and make a profit later down the line), whereas new trendy pieces of furniture usually only lose value over time. Have we convinced you to test out some vintage pieces in your home yet?

- Look for vintage (of course), because it's solid and handmade and, stylistically, has a timeless quality.

- Don't just buy things on a whim for convenience; take a minute to do a little research and see what's available.

- Consider multifunctionality. Could it work in more than one room of your home and grow with you over time?

- Avoid a list of must-get items like "a green sofa." Instead, choose things that are intuitively aesthetically pleasing to you when you discover them and, more than likely, they'll end up working out with whatever else you already have that's true to your style.

- Don't feel pressured to design around a color theme. Let a color story emerge over time as you buy pieces you truly love.

Bringing the Outside In

I CAN'T SAY I HAVE A GREEN THUMB, maybe more of a prickly thumb, as I'm much better at keeping cactuses alive than any other living things. But despite my mediocre horticultural skills, I still love plants and nature deeply, perhaps because I've spent my whole life living either in woodsy areas or just a hop, skip, and jump away from beautiful scenery. When I was a young girl, my little brick home in the English countryside was surrounded on three sides by wheat fields, and I spent hours every day playing in my big backyard while my mom tended to her thriving garden. In junior high and high school, we lived in the Sierra Nevadas of Northern California, and our home was nestled among towering pine trees. You could always hear the rush of Deer Creek flowing and the crickets chirping. Now, having lived in the greater Seattle area for a third of my life, the beauty of the Pacific Northwest has become a deep part of my overall aesthetic and, truly, a part of my heart. I've lived just two blocks from a lake, minutes away from a beach, and surrounded by massive trees, all within city limits here in Seattle. Nature is integral to the city and to my own well-being.

Within my home, nature's influence goes beyond just the plants I've scattered throughout it or the little pots of vegetables and herbs that my husband grows. (I'm always finding a new avocado pit shooting up with leaves in a glass jar in a sunny window in my home. My husband loves tending to plants and bringing greenery and food to life. It's a good thing one of us has a green thumb!) The plants that he cares for are usually ones that need a lot of attention, whereas I prefer cactuses, air plants, vines, and things that grow well in shade and with minimal watering. I may have hidden a few faux plants around my home too; I dare you to try to figure out what's real and what's not!

Along with the fake greenery, a very low-maintenance way that I bring the outdoors in is through natural elements that are, ahem, no longer living.

For some it may feel a bit unsettling to have a skull sitting around your home, but I love collecting antique animal skulls because it reminds me of the desert heat in the Southwest, the rustic sensibilities of the Pacific Northwest, and the comforting warmth of the Midwest where my great-grandfather grew up and where my husband's family is from. A reverence for history, family heritage, and mixing of cultures are major influences in my home styling.

My great-grandfather was half Cherokee, born in Kansas, and raised in a sod house on his father's farm while they built a beautiful wooden farmhouse. My dad and I look a lot like him except for our freckled pale skin. He taught himself how to read by reading the newspapers that lined the interior walls of the sod house. He graduated from the University of Missouri, becoming the youngest judge in Oklahoma history at the age of twenty-seven. He then moved to Long Beach, California, in 1922, where he was both a judge and a prominent attorney. His life story has been a huge catalyst in inspiring my own life's journey. I admire him for pursuing his dreams in an age where he could have easily been held back by others because of the color of his skin, his family heritage, and the place where he grew up. But he pushed through and built a beautiful life for himself while remaining proud of who he was and where he came from. He raised and nurtured five children on his own in the thirties when his wife ran off and abandoned them. And that incredible balance of defying all odds to provide for his family both as the breadwinner and the caregiver is what I seek for myself as well. Though my own brushes with adversity have been so different from his, I still relate to his legacy of giving to others, even while facing his own hardships and living outside of society's expectations. And by decorating my home in ways that reflect my Native American heritage—with rich, warm colors and textures, beautiful patterned textiles, family rugs passed down within my family hanging on my copper ladder, and natural elements from plants to bones and stones—I feel my great-grandfather's presence with me every day.

His daughter, my grandma, kept a lot of his traditions alive within my family, gifting them to my dad and now to me. In many ways, my family can be kind of morbid, but in a respectful, awe-inspired way. My grandparents were—and my parents are—very comfortable talking about the fragility of life, the swiftness of time, and the beauty in the cyclical pattern of life and death. I, too, am pretty comfortable with death, though I have had many traumatic experiences of losing loved ones. By surrounding my home with natural elements like plants whose life spans are far shorter than my own, I feel more comfortable with the transitions within my own life, the moments that come and go and the experiences that only last for a time.

My grandma's ways of honoring life and retaining her adoration for her father and those who appreciate nature were definitely channeled into how she

gave back to others and how she displayed precious objects around her home. She collected an extensive variety of turquoise jewelry, much of which she personally commissioned as her way of supporting Native tribes and respecting the beautiful artistry of Native cultures still vibrant today. I inherited her Zuni fetishes, which are little stone bears traditionally carved by the Zuni tribe in New Mexico and Arizona. Traditionally, there are six different types of fetishes: the bear, mountain lion, badger, wolf, eagle, and mole. Each animal is the guardian of a different part of the world: north, south, east, west, above, and below. My grandma collected the bear, the guardian of the west, the place where she was raised and where she gave back to through many charitable causes. These little stone bears are such special treasures to me, reminding me of her respect for her lineage, her love of wildlife, and her peace within the mysterious and unknown.

Though my life experiences and my pale freckled skin tone are so different from that of many of my ancestors, I hope I can keep some of the traditions of honoring those things that thrive in the wild alive within my home and within my own family for generations to come. On rainy days, of which there are many here in Seattle, I still sometimes sing the rain song that my dad taught me as a little girl, a song that was passed down to him from his mother. My dad says that my great-grandfather would sing it with his father when their crops were dying, praying for rain. And when I was little in England, as we drove to school through farmland and fields, my dad and I would sing our family rain song as a wish for rain for the farmers.

By respecting and honoring my family traditions, loving animals well, bringing plants into my home, and learning from my husband and his love of cultivating a thriving garden and resurrecting dying plants, I am constantly reminded of the importance of nature and how I must nurture and honor myself well. By taking time to try to understand how each plant in my home needs a different type of care, different routines of watering and hours in the sun, I realize that with practice, I can learn personal wellness just as steadily. Natural elements and nature-inspired pieces in my home—like lots of rich wood, a sheepskin draped over my sofa, Native-made rugs from my family, plants everywhere, and my grandma's Zuni fetishes—give me a deep feeling of belonging. And though my animal skulls are a touch cryptic in how they remind me of the fleeting nature of life, they also bring me peace in accepting that life does not go on forever and each moment should—and can—be cherished. I am grateful for the time I have to learn to invest in myself and grateful for the ways I can honor family and nature within my home.

At Home in Your Space

NATURE

Nature is truly magical, and you are a part of it. Don't forget that it takes time and practice to help living things thrive to their full potential. What are a few ways that you like to bring nature into your home? Plants are a simple and straightforward means to liven up a dull space, and beyond their beauty, there is so much to learn about the practice of self-investment through the ritual of tending to plants and their varying needs. But if caring for plants feels too intimidating, you can always start easy, like me, with plants that need little light or watering. Or simply enjoy the beauty and inspiration found in well-made faux greenery scattered around your home or objects that speak to nature or that remind you of life's beautiful, mysterious cycle. Infusing your home with natural elements can be an inspiration to allow yourself to truly live and thrive along with them.

Consider your own space as you ponder these questions. Let your mind wander! Feel free to use the Notes section in the back of the book for journaling or sketching out ideas.

- What mood/vibe/feeling does nature evoke within you?

- What are your favorite memorable moments from time spent in nature?

- What are your favorite colors and textures found in nature?

- What decorative items do you already have that feel inspired by nature?

- What rooms in your home might need that natural touch to feel alive?

FIVE EASY-CARE INDOOR PLANTS

1 **ALOE PLANT:** My mom always kept an aloe plant around our home growing up. It loves sunlight and is easy to care for, and its leaves can be cut off to use the aloe inside to heal wounds, burns, and scrapes! Aloe is my favorite cure for a bad sunburn and is on many windowsills around my home.

   GROWING CONDITIONS: *Medium to bright light. It prefers to be in a window with lots of sunshine but can handle medium light pretty well. Water every two to three weeks, making sure the soil dries out well between waterings. It holds all of its moisture in its leaves, so be sure not to overwater!*

2 **CACTUS:** Cactuses with spines, spikes, bristles, or woolly coverings are easier to keep alive than smooth succulents with wide leaves that need more watering and light. Most cactuses have dormant seasons where they don't need any watering from November through February! Here are a few of my favorite types of easy-to-care-for cactuses: ball cactus, ruby ball cactus, fairy castle cactus, zebra cactus, old man cactus, and pincushion cactus.

   GROWING CONDITIONS: *Low to bright light. Set your cactus in a sunny window for a few hours once a week to keep it happy. Water rarely! Most cactuses have evolved away from having leaves as a way to store all their nutrients as close to their core as possible, making them super durable without much watering. If your home has dry air, water your cactus once every three weeks and make sure the soil dries out for a long time between waterings. I have a few small cactuses that have happily never been watered in a year because they soak up any moisture in the air as needed from steam from showers, boiling water, and air humidifiers.*

3 **PHILODENDRON:** Philodendrons are one of the most classic easy-to-care-for indoor house plants. I love setting them high on a bookcase or shelf, letting their drooping stems grow down the edge of the shelf. They can grow up to eight feet long if you let them!

   GROWING CONDITIONS: *Low to bright light, growing faster in bright light. Water once every one to two weeks, depending on how moist the air is in your home. No need to water too often; just wait and watch for drooping leaves and water as needed. Yellowing and softening of the leaves means you might be overwatering.*

4 **PONYTAIL PALM:** Don't let its name trick you—the ponytail palm is actually a succulent with long hairlike leaves (like a pony!) and a bulbous trunk that stores water. I love imagining this plant with a little sassy personality to match its sassy style.

   GROWING CONDITIONS: *Ideally it gets bright light all year long, but you can get away with bright light for half the year in warmer months and low light in the colder months. Water every two to three weeks. If it develops brown tips on the ends of its leaves, it may need to be watered less or potted in low-quality soil. Avoid high-quality, nutrient-rich soils, as it already has what it needs in its trunk and flushes out water better with low-quality soil.*

5 **SNAKE PLANT:** The snake plant is my favorite go-to plant to add height and structure to a collection of plants. It is super easy to care for and prefers low light, so it's great for shady corners of your home or places where you don't get much natural light.

   GROWING CONDITIONS: *Low to bright light. It grows faster the brighter the light. Water once every two to three weeks, similar to a cactus. It holds a lot of moisture in its leaves, so allow the soil surface to dry between watering. If the tips of the leaves feel soft and damp, give it some time to really dry out before you water again.*

◄ SNAKE PLANT

▼ PHILODENDRON

CACTUS ►

PONYTAIL PALM ►

◄ ALOE

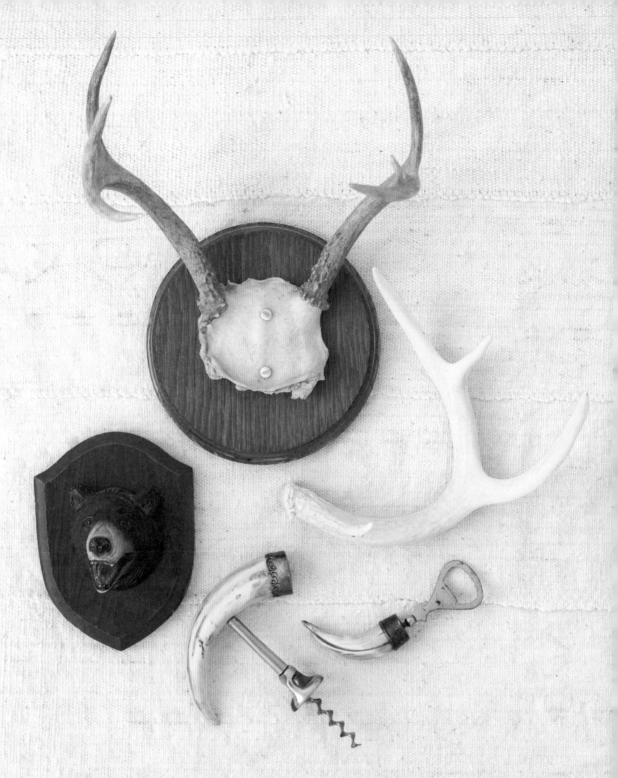

Plants can be intimidating to those who have never cared for them before or who seem to lack a green thumb. No worries! There are lots of ways to bring nature into your home that don't involve tending to the needs of plants. Here are my favorite ways to bring the outside in without much upkeep.

TEN NATURAL ELEMENTS YOU DON'T HAVE TO WATER

1. Add crystals to a tabletop or dresser to bring a natural and more bohemian, mystical vibe to your space. Some people believe in healing powers of crystals; try an amethyst for feelings of protection and spirituality, citrine for emotional balance and cleansing, jade for prosperity and longevity, or kyanite for clear communication and meditative focus.

2. Display wall art inspired by nature, like a photograph of a place you love.

3. Hang a thick branch from two wires in your ceiling and use it as a clothing rack or a place to display your favorite necklaces.

4. Hide fake plants in areas where you aren't tempted to look too closely at the leaves' details. (I have a fake air plant hidden in a hanging plant holder in my dining room.)

5. Add a few pinecones to a table next to your sofa or along your windowsill. I love keeping pinecones around my home as a way to keep the feeling of fall alive in my house year-round.

6. Go on an adventure and create a collection of natural objects that you find on your journey—whether you go for a walk down your street or on a tropical vacation. Look for rocks, shells from the beach, dried leaves in every color of the rainbow, or acorns from a nearby tree to hold in a beautiful bowl on a tabletop.

7. Take a note from grandma: stash a sachet of lavender buds in a drawer in your dresser to keep your clothes smelling fresh.

8. Decorate your walls with a plant-patterned wallpaper! My friend Justina Blakeney has a beautiful line of home goods and wallpaper covered in her gorgeous, "jungalow"-inspired artwork.

9. Use antlers as decorative objects around your home.

10. Use a wood stump as a side table.

Make: MOON PHASE WALL HANGING

Add a touch of celestial inspiration to your home with this pretty moon phase wall hanging. There are tons of ways to make this DIY unique to you—with color or your choice of sizes for each moon phase piece. Feel free to experiment and see what feels most special to you!

STEPS

1. Tape a large square piece of cellophane onto the mat.

2. Break off a piece of polymer clay about the size of a fist and roll it into a ball in your hands. Repeat this with four more balls of clay.

3. On the cellophane-covered mat, roll out the clay balls with a rolling pin into circles or, for a more organic look, use your hands to flatten them evenly. They don't have to be perfect, just big enough to fit the round cookie cutter.

4. Use the round cookie cutter to cut out four circles of clay, or place your paper circle template on top of one of the circles of clay and, using an X-Acto knife, cut the circle shape out of the clay. Use the star-shaped cookie cutter to cut out one star, or place your paper star template on top of one of the circles of clay and, using an X-Acto knife, cut the star shape out of the clay.

5. Keep one clay cutout circle as your top "full" moon.

6. Take three clay circles and, using the X-Acto knife or cookie cutter, cut a different-sized crescent-shaped moon out of each to represent the waxing/waning phases of the moon, from a half moon to a smaller crescent. To get varied crescent moon shapes, just press the cutter in a little lower into the clay circle.

7. Preheat the oven to 275 degrees F.

8. Let the clay shapes cool for a few minutes after being worked with your warm hands.

MATERIALS AND TOOLS

Tape

Cellophane or cling wrap

Self-healing mat

1 (1.75-pound) package white polymer clay

Rolling pin (optional)

Round cookie cutter, 1–4 inches in diameter (or cut a piece of paper in the shape of a circle to use as a template, see page 150)

Star-shaped cookie cutter, 1–4 inches in diameter (or cut a piece of paper in the shape of a star to use as a template, see page 150)

X-Acto knife

Toothpick or diffuser stick

Ovenproof glass baking pan or baking sheet

Oven

Metallic acrylic paint (optional)

1 (6-inch) piece malleable wire (you could also try using a yarn needle, or use a toothpick or diffuser stick to push the twine through the holes)

. . . continued

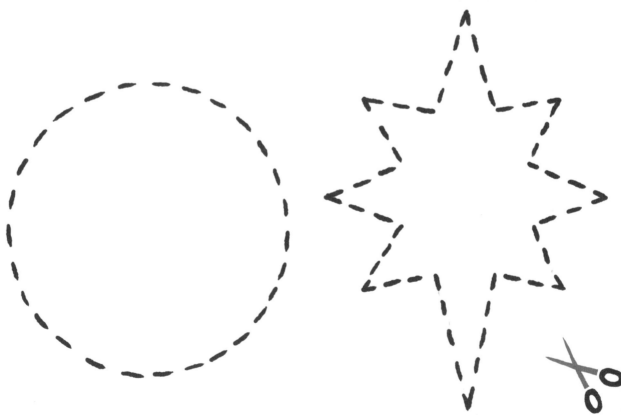

9. Use a toothpick or diffuser stick to poke a hole in the top and bottom of each clay moon and the top of the star. This is where you will attach the twine between each moon shape, so make sure the holes are big enough to fit the twine through.

10. Bake the clay shapes on an ovenproof glass pan or baking sheet, following your polymer clay package directions (my Sculpey clay called for 15 minutes at 275 degrees F).

11. Let the clay pieces cool for at least 30 minutes after baking.

12. Paint each piece however you like. I prefer to keep mine in the original white because I like that rustic, natural look. If you paint them, let the paint dry for about 3 hours before adding the twine.

13. Wrap a piece of wire around the end of the twine. It will act as your needle.

14. Cut a 6-inch piece of twine and loop it through the holes in the clay pieces, first connecting the full circle and the half circle, tying it off with a knot in the back. Allow about 2 inches between the shapes. Repeat, connecting the rest of the moon shapes in descending size, with the star at the bottom.

15. Cut an 8-inch piece of twine and, using the wire to thread it, create a loop through the top of the round circle (the full moon), tying it off with a knot in the back. This is the loop you will use to hang it vertically from a nail in the wall.

Scissors

Baker's twine (if you'd like the shapes to appear as if they're floating, use a thinner material like fishing wire or brass wire; I prefer the chunkier, rustic look of the twine)

Nail and hammer

For information on where to buy materials and tools, see Resources (page 185).

VARIATION: PLAY WITH COLOR

Mix black and white polymer clay to create a marbled effect, or fold in different metallic acrylic paints. Once your clay has baked, you can paint directly onto it using a paintbrush. The color options are endless with mixing clay or painting!

Make: NATURE GALLERY WALL

Hanging art can seem tricky—but it doesn't have to be! This technique will allow you to try out different spacing and placing of your favorite pieces before you commit to drilling through your wall. Have fun with it! No one says you need to hang everything in straight lines.

STEPS

1. Gather the artwork and objects that you want to use for your gallery wall.

2. Lay each piece on the paper and trace their shapes onto the paper.

3. Cut out each paper shape.

4. Create hanging marks on each piece of paper to show where you will need to put a hole in the wall for each piece of art. Put the paper on top of the back of your art piece and put a mark where the nail should go or at the hardware piece where some frames have a place to hang your art built in, on the bottom of the frame's top edge. For art hung with wire, with the wire already attached to the back of your frame, flip the frame over and use a ruler to measure the center of the frame between the left and right side. Mark the center by drawing a vertical line from the center of the frame to the top of the frame. Then, using your pointer finger, pull the wire up the back of the frame, drawing your finger along the center line that you just created. Once you can't pull your finger any farther up the frame, mark this spot, along the center line, as your nail point on the frame itself. Mark this same spot on the paper template.

MATERIALS AND TOOLS

Artwork

Large roll of kraft or butcher paper, or newspaper (as wide as your largest piece of art, or you can tape 2 pieces together)

Pencil

Scissors

Masking tape

Nails or picture-hanging hardware

Hammer

Level or level smartphone app

Ruler (optional)

For information on where to buy materials and tools, see Resources (page 185).

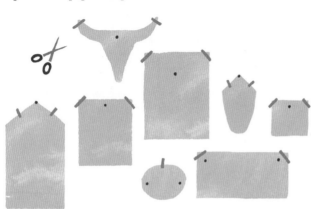

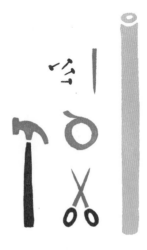

. . . *continued*

5. Add a piece of tape to each paper shape and use the paper cutouts as a way to map out your gallery of images on your wall!

6. You can arrange and rearrange as much as you like, playing with spacing and organization, until you are ready to replace the paper tracing by nailing the actual piece of art or object to the wall. If you like, use a ruler to measure the space between templates, and a level to make sure they are hanging straight.

7. Hammer the nail directly through the nail mark on your paper template when you're ready to hang! Then you can just rip the paper off, replacing the template with the framed art, one at a time. Use a level to straighten each frame.

8. Check out the tips below for inspiration on how to choose art, frames, and more!

GALLERY WALL TIPS

Choosing a Color Palette

When it comes to color for a gallery wall, it's all or nothing! The easiest way to make a lot of pieces of art look good together is to go either very colorful or very subtle in tones and colors. For my wall, I went with all black and white to match the desks in our office and to keep the space feeling tidy and clean. I love the look of a space that has only black and white images. But I also love the opposite, a wall filled with color. If you're going to go wild with the amount of art on the wall, you might as well go a little wild as well with your theme or color palette! See At Home with Color (page 168) to discover complementary colors.

Choosing Frames

I recommend sticking to a theme when it comes to choosing frames. If you like a clean and modern vibe, choose frames that are nice and linear, clean and smooth, and matching in shape. Ikea is my go-to for affordable frames with clean lines. But if you are going for a more eclectic look, opt for a wide variety of frames where most do not match. Hunting thrift stores for frames is an easy and affordable way to find a quirky assortment of unique frames in all shapes and sizes!

Choosing a Theme

Generally, a gallery wall looks best when there is some sort of theme, be it subtle or loud. My gallery wall is a mixture of plant life and girl power, a balance of approachable nature and in-your-face lady pride. I love the look of a wall of just black-and-white photography, or one that is all portraits. A wall that has a mixture of rustic or bohemian paintings, drawings, and eclectic objects always makes for a stunning display. A wall of art that is all of the same genre or era is a classic way to display art as well. (My parents both love fine art and my dad has collected postimpressionist California art for the latter part of his life and displays it on gallery walls.)

Beginning Your Arrangement

I always like to start with three frames as the center of my arrangement. I usually choose two large and one smaller frame to add dimension. And once I like how the three look together, I build off that focal point, adding art around the grouping of three until it feels full and balanced overall. Practice adding the pieces of paper to the wall, then turning around and walking away, trying to forget how the arrangement first looked. Then from afar, turn around and view the overall look with clear eyes. Do this a few times with a few different arrangements and take photos of each arrangement to compare and contrast your favorites to make your final decision.

Going Beyond Framed Art

A gallery wall doesn't have to include just drawings, paintings, posters, and photography. Try adding unique natural objects to your gallery wall to create a richer textured landscape to your collection. My rule of thumb is that if you are going to add unique objects to a gallery wall of art, if the objects are smaller, make sure you have at least three objects. One or two objects can look really lonely without some friends. Hang a feather, a butterfly specimen, and beautiful leaf or shell amid your art to add a little more nature. If you are going to bring in just one larger object, either make it the center point of your gallery wall or add it at the top of your gallery wall. Something that works well like this is a bull skull for a Western-inspired touch.

GETTING GREEN WITH
Laura Gummerman

LAURA GUMMERMAN

Blogger at A Beautiful Mess

LIVES IN: Nashville, Tennessee

FROM: Pittsburgh, Pennsylvania

SIGNATURE STYLE: rock 'n' roll meets Palm Springs

HOW SHE BECAME A BLOGGER: Sometimes simply doing what you love, without any ulterior motive, can bring great rewards. Laura has had her own blog for some time, documenting her life as a "band wife," her husband being one of the members of the band Mutemath. During one of his tours on the road, she renovated their entire house on her own, and her close friend Elsie, the founder of *A Beautiful Mess*, took notice of Laura's incredible self-motivation and artistic skills, and she invited Laura to join the *Beautiful Mess* crew. Laura contributes there, among many things, some of the best DIY projects across the web. I guarantee that a ton of the DIYs you have pinned to your Pinterest boards were created by her!

WHAT SHE LOVES: plants (duh!), particularly cactuses, palms, and tropical plants; stark white walls; pops of pastels like pink accent walls; pop-art murals and neon signs in small but impactful doses; eclectic DIY plant containers; natural elements like fur and hides; midcentury modern accents; artwork that celebrates summer and the outdoors

I first discovered Laura Gummerman and her incredible DIY talents through my friend Elsie's blog, *A Beautiful Mess*. I deeply admire Laura's crafting, building, and innovation prowess—along with the fact that she exudes confidence while being super down-to-earth and kind-spirited. Her charm and relaxed attitude are effortlessly conveyed not only in how she styles herself but also how she styles her space, playing with pops of pastels and neon colors against clean, neutral bases. Our home-décor styles are almost entirely opposite, mine being more warm-toned and darker while hers is cool-toned and bright. But in those styles, our unique vibes and passions are translated clearly, me loving the richness and

coziness of fall and winter, bringing warmth into my home through reds, browns, and oranges, and Laura celebrating the freshness and light of spring and summer, using white and bright blues and pinks. But one thing we do have in common is our obsession with plants! When it comes to inspiration, we both love feeling the energy that living plants give off in our homes. And it's fascinating for me to see some of the ways she styles her plants differently than I do within her home. I discover some of my greatest motivation in my own creative pursuits by learning from and observing people whose aesthetic and style are different from my own. And over the years, I feel like I've learned so much of what it means to be true to yourself by just watching incredible women like Laura through their blogging and creative expression. Her home is one of my favorites ever, and I

know it's because it's an honest and true reflection of what brings her joy.

LAURA'S INDOOR JUNGLE

Laura and her husband recently moved to Nashville and bought a sixties ranch-style house that allows her to indulge her love of a retro Palm Springs aesthetic and to play around with her quirky, truly one-of-a-kind knack for blurring the lines between indoors and outdoors. While she painted her patio to look like black-and-white tiles reminiscent of something you might more commonly find in a kitchen, inside her house is full of greenery, from towering cactuses taking center stage to smaller arrangements grouped intimately together on shelves, next to a piano, tucked between soap dispensers, even displayed in the

hollowed-out center of a vintage telephone. "There's not a spot that's off-limits!" she says. "I'll put them on my bar cart . . . I can't really think of where I *wouldn't* put one. You just kind of get this feeling . . . that there's a dead zone when plants aren't there."

Besides plants, she also brings the outdoors in via leaf-patterned wallpaper, a sun-shaped ceiling fixture, big, bold photographs of cactuses and beach scenes, nature-inspired colors like ocean-toned teal, and furry rugs and pillows. This all works especially well with her beachy yet sophisticated California vibe that, ironically, doesn't come from actually having spent much time there. Instead, she credits the influence of popular culture. "I grew up on sixties movies, so I've always loved that mod vibe in general, but the cheerful sunny California twist on the whole thing is right up my alley. I

like to give the Palm Springs nod in my home décor through the desert-inspired plants and artwork, and most of the furniture is a replica or inspired by the sleek midcentury designs as well. We also have lots of globe and Sputnik-type lighting fixtures all over the house that complement the feel of that era. Our house is a sixties ranch, so it all goes together nicely from the outside in and I actually just planted prickly pear and fan palms in the front yard, and I can't wait to watch them grow! I even made a Palm Springs cat house for our kitties. Since I don't want the house to look like a total time capsule, I've also added in a few other details to modernize the feel. Lots of gold accents, pastels, neon signs, and a few other quirky items to make the space feel more unique. I like to think that if Nasty Gal had a house in Palm Springs, it would look sort of like mine!"

HOW BRINGING THE OUTDOORS IN REFLECTS—AND AFFECTS—LAURA'S LIFE AND MOOD

Laura credits both her mother and her father for her love of warmth and the outdoors. Her dad was a teacher, so summer became her favorite season because he was home every day and it was all about ice cream, playing, and constant fun. Meanwhile, her mother is a true green thumb and Laura's go-to person for anything plant-related. "I have memories of her tending to her plants day after day in the summers. Sometimes she would even be out there at midnight under the floodlights planting while the temperature was nice and cool! I actually waited until she could help me pick out plants in person before landscaping our last backyard—I didn't want to do it without the pro!"

"You just kind of get this feeling . . . that there's a dead zone when plants aren't there."

After growing up in Pittsburgh, Laura was definitely over the cold and dark days that winter would bring. Even in a southern state, Laura still doesn't love when the weather starts to cool and fall and winter approach. She believes that when a house looks tropical and desertlike, it makes you feel happy even when there's ten feet of snow outside. She is all about keeping the inside of her home fresh, vibrant, and buzzing with life to combat the ever-changing seasons, almost as if her home is an eternal summer. And when it comes to decorating, plants are the easiest way she has found to bring life and vibrancy indoors. "Because plants actually are alive, they give off a totally different vibe than a coffee-table book or decorative objects," she says. "It's like we're all sharing the space together. I worry about them if they aren't doing well, and it makes me so happy to see new leaves and growth when they are happy."

LAURA'S GREEN JOURNEY

Despite the effortless look of her home—and its chic yet desert-inspired feel—Laura admits that her creative use of nature in her space didn't come, er, naturally. You certainly wouldn't guess it by the looks of her home, but she's actually a recent plant convert. "I think I always assumed plants were for old ladies or dentists' offices, but then I started to notice that there were a lot of modern, fresh, young-looking spaces where the plants were some of the coolest things in the room," she says. "Now I'm a bit of an addict and I love collecting all different varieties. Plants bring so much life to a space (probably because they are alive—duh!), so if there's an area or corner that is feeling visually dull, plants are usually the answer." She loves the bird of paradise palm, but her current favorite is the *Monstera* plant because of its amazing "swiss cheese" leaves. Cactuses are another favorite. She even has a six-foot-tall cactus in her den that kills her every time she sees it. Why cactus? As Laura says, "they're easier to take care of (yes, even easier than succulents!), they grow like crazy when you move them outside in the summer, and they can add a lot of dramatic height. They're the badass plants of nature; they would wear a leather jacket if they could." Just like Laura herself, who feels most comfortable in a good leather moto jacket (but in the perfect pastel pink) with edgy pumps that make a statement. With her chic rocker look, love of summer and sunshine, laid-back attitude, and fierce independence, Laura seems like she grew up in California just like me! She created her own oasis within her home to reflect her true self, a powerhouse of upbeat energy and personality.

LAURA'S TIPS
for Decorating with Plants

When I was a college student, I had one or two plants at a time, which suited my tiny budget. I usually had one plant for just having a plant's sake, but didn't think about creating a home for it within my own home. Once you can figure out how to create thoughtful spaces for your plants, you'll start to feel yourself come alive from the good vibes that plants add to your home. Just like you are living in a space that suits you, plants need to live in a space that suits them. Check out Laura's tips for giving more purpose to the placement of your plants in your home.

- Like any other decorating choice in a house, plant placement is all about balance. They should be evenly sprinkled through a room without feeling too plant-heavy in only one area (although an exception can be made for a plant-patterned wallpaper covering a wall or any other major plant statement centered in a space).

- Variety! It's important to have lots of different sizes and scales as well as types to keep the space feeling fresh. Spread the plant love across your home, hanging from wall planters, perched on tabletops, in big pots on the floor. Really large plants tend to look best by themselves dominating one area of a room, while small and medium plants of different heights and widths look better together in groups of three or five, on a mantel or shelf.

- Make sure your plant not only fits the area but will also get the right amount of light. There are so many times I want to put a plant somewhere, but I just can't because the light conditions aren't right and it won't survive.

- Use lots of hanging plants and wall planters. They are lots of fun!

- If something looks lonely, add a plant next to it.

- Take simple, inexpensive risks. Wallpaper can be an expensive mistake if you don't like it, so I did removable wallpaper for my palm print. Or try a DIY plant stand or container.

Acknowledgments

I WOULD LIKE TO THANK Nicole Sprinkle for her help in creating structure around my creativity, taking our interview sessions and transforming them into concise stories, and working away with me as we tested and experimented with DIYs.

Thank you to the six amazing women who were kind enough to let us share a bit of their stories and see beautiful moments within their homes.

Thank you to Marissa Maharaj for her gorgeous photography work and for being the best travel buddy and photoshoot friend a girl could ask for.

Thank you to Julia Manchik whose illustrations are perfect representations of the emotions of home and whose work on all three of my books has been irreplaceable.

Thank you to my husband for being down with allowing the world a peek into our shared space and for cultivating a home with depth alongside me.

Thank you to my live-in middle sister, Alexandra, whose adaptability, unique voice, and kindness while living with her big sister and her brother-in-law has been essential to building a full home together. Thank you to my youngest sister, Isabella, the wild and powerful mama lion who has inspired me beyond words in her growth in motherhood and her true definition of what it means to be and find home.

Thank you to so many friends and women I adore who inspire the pursuit of self-care, respect, love, creativity, strength, power, peace, energy, community, and wellness: Allie F., Amy M., Melissa M., Kim K., Laura L., Andrea C-H., Beca S., Katie D., Rebecca C., Morgan S., Melissa B-W., Laura M., Shanley K., Liz M., Kaelah B., Kara H., Lindsey D., Jessy O., Sierra H., Kimberly J., Julie S., Erin P., Molly M., Sarah R., Margaret J., Brandy B., Capri W., Kelly-Ann M., Laura B., Katy S., Tammy T., Aidyn S., Sarah C., Brenna M., Jen S., Diana L., and Sarah S.

Thank you to the whole crew on my staff for your patience with me in my quirky creative ways and your belief in me as a boss and a maker. I truly wouldn't be able to do anything I do without your presence and power on our team: Reed, Jenette, Tram, Jessie, and the whole gang.

Lastly, thank you to everyone at Sasquatch Books and Random House for your belief in my vision of each book that I've had the privilege to write and for all your hard work in bringing my ideas and stories to life.

At Home with Color

COLOR THEORY FOR HOME

You have probably seen this wheel before, back when you were first learning about color in kindergarten or middle school. Well, the theories you were introduced to then still apply now! And we can use insights found in color theory to create the mood and feelings that you desire in each of your spaces.

Primary Colors
RED BLUE YELLOW

Red, blue, and yellow are the only **THREE** colors that cannot be created by blending other colors together. When standing alone and in their most concentrated form, these colors can be very visually dominant.

Secondary Colors
ORANGE PURPLE GREEN

Orange, purple, and green are the **THREE** colors that are created by blending two primary colors: red + yellow = orange, red + blue = purple, and blue + yellow = green.

Tertiary Colors

SIX tertiary colors are created by blending a primary color and a secondary hue (a hue is a color that has not had any white or black added to it, just a blending of pure colors). Notice a teal tone is created by blending green, a secondary color, and blue, a primary color; both are located on either side of teal on the color wheel.

These twelve colors are the source of infinite new color variations. If these colors are used together in a space in your home, though, it might get a little intense, as each color is so dense and vibrant. My trick is to choose at least one of these colors as a focus for a space (whether you choose a more muted and subtle variation of these colors is up to you), but to use that color sparingly as a focus and pop in your space. To fill out that picture, let's get to know the difference between hue, tint, shade, and tone to help you better envision what sort of level of saturation you like best in colors in your home.

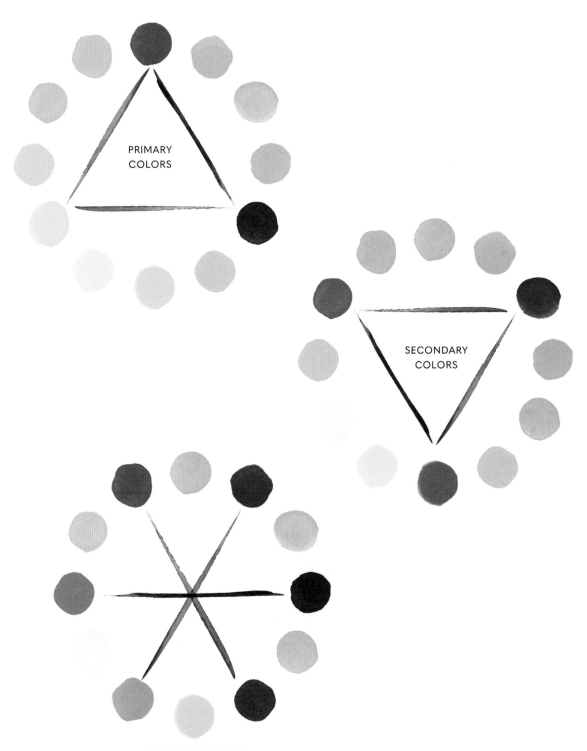

PRIMARY
COLORS

SECONDARY
COLORS

TERTIARY COLORS

Hue, Tint, Shade, or Tone?

HUE: Hues are the twelve brightest and purest colors found in the primary, secondary, and tertiary color wheels. These are a great launching point for the sorts of colors you are attracted to, but use them sparingly—that is, unless you want your space to be screaming with color and vibrancy!

TINT: A tint is any color or color combination with white added. Tinting is an easy way to simply lighten a color, but the more white you add to your color, the less vibrant and the more pastel your color will become. In a space where a lot of pastels or pale colors are used, white tends to blend smoothly and softly.

SHADE: A shade is any color or color combination with black added. Black tends to suck a lot of the color out of a space or wherever it is used. And that same thing happens when blending black with colors. Color becomes muted and moody very quickly as soon as black is added. The same goes for a space; if you have a black wall in your home, adding color in front of the wall will be a less intense change than if you add lots of colors in front of a white wall or a pastel wall. The colors tend to retreat into the dark, whereas colors surrounded by light tend to pop.

TONE: A tone is any color with a touch of white and black (gray) added. The paint chips you see at your local hardware or paint store are most often tones of colors, which are often the easiest to work with in a space. The touch of black softens and dilutes the color to be easier on the eye, and the white adds a touch of calming softness and lightness. In decorating, choosing colors that are in a family of analogous tones is an easy way to add variety into your space without overwhelming it.

Analogous Colors

Analogous colors are found next to each other on the color wheel and are most similar in color. Notice how each color feels a little more calm and peaceful when it's next to colors that are related, while on its own, each color is still very saturated and vibrant.

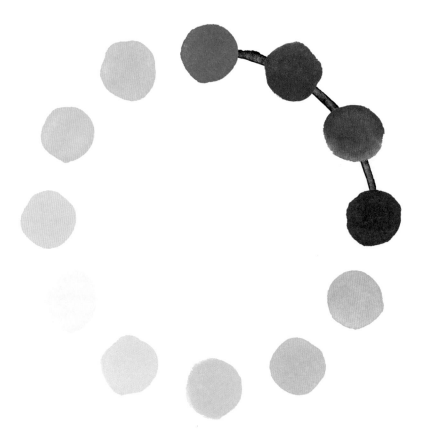

Active and Passive Colors

Most colors that are warmer, on the left side of the color wheel, appear to pop forward when placed next to the colors on the right side of the wheel. In turn, the colors on the right appear to recede. This phenomenon is referred to as active colors versus passive colors. Warm, light, and saturated hues tend to pop, while cool, dark, and desaturated hues tend to recede into the background.

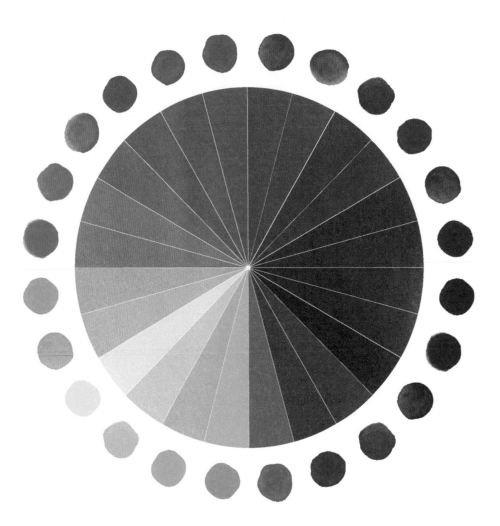

Complementary Colors

To choose colors for your space that will pop and add high contrast, choose complementary colors. Complementary colors are colors that are on opposite sides of the color wheel (e.g., red and green, yellow and purple, orange and blue). You will notice in the photograph of me in my bedroom (see page 112) that my orange-toned dress pops against the dark wall that has touches of deep blue and black. That vibrant contrast is created by complementary colors. Where else do you see that sort of pop of color happening in this book or in your home? And do you like it? Or do you prefer more subtle color variations created with tints, shades, and tones?

COLOR ASSOCIATION

What associations do you already have with the different colors? Which ones seem more energizing and which ones seem more soothing? Which ones are your favorites?

Are there colors that feel inviting and comforting? You may want to use these in your living room. Are there colors that make you feel organized and focused? You may want to use these in your office. Remember, there's no one right answer, it's all about what mood you want to set in each room and how the colors make you feel! But if you're interested in color psychology, see page 176 for what other people have to say about colors!

Red

....
....
....
....
....
....

Yellow

....
....
....
....
....
....

Blue

....
....
....
....
....
....

Orange

....
....
....
....
....
....

Green

....
....
....
....
....
....

Purple

....
....
....
....
....
....

White

Gold

Teal

....
....
....
....
....
....

Black

Brown

Lime

....
....
....
....
....
....

Gray

Maroon

Olive

....
....
....
....
....
....

Silver

Pink

Navy

....
....
....
....
....
....

COLOR PSYCHOLOGY

Color psychology comes into play in so many spaces that you may not even realize it! Did you know that yellow and red are often used in fast-food industry advertising because those are the colors we most intuitively associate with being hungry or having desire? Which fast-food giant has a big yellow and red logo? The logo of most banks and financial institutions are blue, navy, and green and often a combo of blue and red. Blue is often associated with peacefulness, calm, and trust. Navy is commonly associated with security, authority, and duty. Green is an easy association given the color of most paper money in the United States, and has an intuitive connection to growth, wealth, and safety. And when red interacts with blue, it is often a sign of power, determination, and strength. The most common associations with color listed below are not true for everyone, but my bet is that when you start to think about how you feel about each color, you might find some connections.

An interesting test: Try grouping the apps on your phone by the color of their logos. Do you see any common themes among color groups? How do they relate to the words listed below?

Red
Hot • Rebellious • Powerful
Dangerous • Fast • Love
Passionate • Intense
Determined • Strong

Green
Natural • Money
Control • Environmental
Growth • Profit • Jealous
Safety • Spring

Orange
Fall • Warm • Sunset • Tasty
Friendly • Thoughtful
Invigorating • Abrasive
Unpredictable • Mellow

Blue
Peaceful • Centered • Calming
Patient • Communicative
Organized • Freedom • Trust
Smart • Clean • Progress

Yellow
Happy • Energetic • Active
Positive • Cheerful
Bubbly • Jubilant
Fun • Youthful • Summer

Purple
Decadent • Mystical
Royal • Elegant • Vanity
Romantic • Full
Magic • Sensual

White

Clean • Simple • Soft
Pure • Light • New
Fresh • Empty • Winter

Black

Hard • Solid • Stern
Stoic • Mean • Serious
Elegant • Classic • Chic

Gray

Gloomy • Old • Dismal
Lonely • Melancholy
Still • Somber • Corporate
Sad • Empty • Absent • Quiet

Silver

Smooth • Down to Earth • Antique
Cautious • Inviting
Lonely • Generic • Modern
Passive

Gold

Rich • Warm • Lush
Mellow • Refined • Elegant
Luxurious • Elevated

Brown

Rustic • Earthy • Warm
Simple • Natural • Inviting
Calm • Basic • Gentle • Rich

Maroon

Romantic • Passion • War
Hurt • Love • Skepticism
Distrust • Old

Pink

Young • Playful • Happy
Sweet • Vanity • Cute
Silly • Amusing • Beauty
Romantic • Alive

Teal

Calming • Therapeutic
Melancholy • Peaceful • Lazy
Comfort • Easy • Relaxed

Lime

Fresh • Young
Easy • Eager • New
Progress • Bouncy

Olive

Earthy • Rustic • Old
Natural • Organic • Dirty
Disgust • Shabby

Navy

Royal • Corporate
Trust • Authority
Duty • Conservative
Secure • Sharp

At Home with Style

SELF-EXPLORATION CAN BE A STYLISH ENDEAVOR! By learning more about who we are and what inspires us in our personal lives, what stories from our past help to define the people that we are today, and what dreams we have for our future, the easier it is to find deeper connections to specific designs and styles in the spaces around us, even down to what we wear. Here are a few styles of home décor featured in this book. Which vibes behind each style resonate most deeply with you?

FOLK

The core to folk style in home, music, and so much more is the story behind the art. Folk-inspired styling is all about collecting objects and décor that have special meaning, stories, and sentimental value. Try creating a vignette of treasures from your family or adventures you've been on!

RUSTIC

Anything that reminds you of the great outdoors and a warm wood cabin is core to rustic design. Antlers, cowhides, and lots of rich raw wood are often found in rustic homes. Try throwing a sheepskin over your sofa and using a tree stump as a side table to add a touch of rustic flair to your home.

SOUTHWESTERN

Southwestern design is quite obviously inspired by the Southwest in the United States; the honoring of traditional Native American and Mexican textiles, motifs, and design styles; and the dry cactus-laden landscape of Arizona, New Mexico, and Texas. Try adding clay pottery, cactus, and a Mexican blanket to your space to channel a rich Southwestern vibe.

RETRO

Retro design technically refers to anything made within the last ten to fifty years. But nowadays most people use the term when referring to the mass-produced, popular, and colorful design of the '50s, '60s, and '70s, or to describe spaces that seek to truly reflect décor of the past. Rather than sprinkling in a few vintage pieces of furniture in a mostly modern space, retro design is all about replicating a different era as much as you can!

MIDCENTURY MODERN

Midcentury modern–style of furniture design took off in the 1930s and lasted well into the 1960s. In the last ten years, midcentury modern furniture has become highly coveted as the design balances well with almost all other styles of home décor with its clean, crisp lines, smooth curves, slightly rounded edges, and lack of any embellishments.

At Home with Vintage Eras

WHEN EXPLORING VINTAGE FURNITURE DESIGN, it's all about discovering not only what styles you like visually, but what narrative behind each design ethos truly suits you. Midcentury modern design of the 1950s resonates with many people because of its simple lines, clean surfaces, and chic practicality. Because of its lack of any ornamentation, many people love using midcentury modern pieces as a base for a space. It's simple, tasteful, and easy to design around. If you have a more playful attitude, the fun, quirky style of the '60s might catch your fancy as it was highly influenced by pop culture and pop art of the time, and if you dig a more refined but charming vibe, art deco might be calling your name. Zen goddesses tend to gravitate to the ornate yet natural essence of bohemian design, cultivated in the '70s. And the more serious and austere find peace in the architecturally influenced minimalism and elegant lines of Bauhaus design. Make your space uniquely you by combining a few vintage eras to reflect the complex and unique characteristics of who you are.

CHAIRS THROUGH THE DECADES

1910: ART NOUVEAU

the marquetry chair

STYLE: highly decorative, elongated, and curved shapes

MATERIALS: high-polished wood and luxury veneers

MOOD: formal, poised, complex

1920: ART DECO

the club chair

STYLE: decorative and glamorous

MATERIALS: gold plated metal and velvet

MOOD: charming, cheeky, elegant

1930: BAUHAUS

the wassily chair

STYLE: minimalist and architectural

MATERIALS: steel and leather

MOOD: serious, practical, refined

1940: UTILITARIAN

the workman's stool

STYLE: industrial and practical

MATERIALS: steel and affordable wood

MOOD: sensible, pragmatic, gritty

1950: MIDCENTURY MODERN

the eames chair

STYLE: accessible design inspired by clean, organic shapes

MATERIALS: teak wood, steel, and fiberglass

MOOD: tasteful, balanced, tidy

1960: MOD

the egg/bubble chair

STYLE: pop art, rounded, and bright colors

MATERIALS: fiberglass and leather

MOOD: playful, unconventional, energetic

1970: BOHEMIAN

the peacock chair

STYLE: world influenced, decorative, folksy, and textured

MATERIALS: rattan

MOOD: peaceful, free-spirited, down to earth

Resources

Select retailers are listed here, but most of the following supplies can be purchased through Amazon.

DIY PROJECTS

Copper Blanket Ladder

¾-inch copper piping, ¾-inch copper pressure tees, and ¾-inch copper end caps:
Home Depot and Lowe's

Essential Oil Diffuser

Hosley's Set of 4 Square Glass Diffuser Bottles, Silky Scent's Amber essential oil, and Hosley's Set of 100 8.75-Inch Rattan Diffuser Reeds:
TheHosleyStore.com

Rocky Mountain Oil's essential oils in blend of rose; vetiver; bergamot; patchouli; Bulgaria or Hungary lavender; and eucalyptus citriodora, eucalyptus globulus, or eucalyptus radiate:
RockyMountainOils.com

Pure Body Naturals Sweet Almond Oil (do not use if you are allergic to nuts) and Art Naturals Fractionated Coconut Oil:
Trader Joe's or Whole Foods

Herb Drying Rack

Cayman Kitchen Natural Cotton Cooking Twine

Medium clothespins and 12-inch embroidery hoop:
Jo-Ann Fabric and Craft Stores

Floral Ice Cubes

Edible flowers:
PCC Natural Market, local florists, or specialty supermarkets

Arctic Chill Large Ice Cube Tray

Gold-Patterned Glassware

Taylor'd Milestones Scotch Glasses

Sharpie Oil-Based Extra-Fine-Point Gold Paint Marker:
Michaels or local art stores

Macramé Wall Hanging

DMC embroidery floss in Golden Brown 976, LT Beaver Gray 648, Satin Blue S414, and V DK Gray Green 924, and 3- and 5-inch embroidery hoops:
Jo-Ann Fabric and Craft Stores

Ikea Desk Hack

28-inch Round Taper Table Leg and Angle Top Plates (with screws):
WaddellMFG.com

Varathane Dark Walnut Wood Stain:
Home Depot

Linnmon Ikea Tabletop:
Ikea

Marbled Leather Mouse Pad

Thick leather, faux leather, or
upholstery vinyl:
**Jo-Ann Fabric and Craft Stores, most
fabric stores, or leather stores**

Fiskars 18-by-24-inch Self-Healing Mat:
**Jo-Ann Fabric and Craft Stores or other
craft stores**

Krylon spray paint in navy and copper:
**Jo-Ann Fabric and Craft Stores, other
craft stores, or Home Depot**

North Star Mirror

6-inch frameless round glass mirror

24-gauge dead-soft brass wire:
Craft or bead stores

Copper Pipe Necklace Display

½-inch copper pipe, ½-inch copper pressure
tees and end caps, ½-inch copper pressure
(or male adapter), ½-inch iron floor flange,
and wood block:
**Home Depot, Lowe's, or local
hardware stores**

Moon Phase Wall Hanging

Fiskars 18-by-24-inch Self-Healing Mat:
**Jo-Ann Fabric and Craft Stores or other
craft stores**

Sculpey White Original Polymer Clay:
Jo-Ann Fabric and Craft Stores

Krylon metallic acrylic paint:
**Jo-Ann Fabric and Craft Stores, Home
Depot, or other craft stores**

Baker's twine

Nature Gallery Wall

Honeymoon Hotel:
HoneymoonHotel.Etsy.com

Alemi Prints:
AlemiPrints.Etsy.com

Maja Plugoleck:
MajaMade.com

HOME GOODS

Although some of the pieces photographed
in the book are family heirlooms or vintage
finds, you can also find many at the following
stores, including chains, online stores, and
local boutiques, in Seattle and across the
United States.

- **Moorea Seal** (MooreaSeal.com or my
  storefront in Seattle)

- **Etsy** (Etsy.com)

- **West Elm** (WestElm.com)

- **Cost Plus World Market**
  (WorldMarket.com)

- **Ikea** (Ikea.com)

- **Target** (Target.com)

- **Amazon** (Amazon.com)

- **D+K Renewal**
  (DKRenewal.bigcartel.com)

- **Kitkitdizzi** (Kitkitdizzi.com or the
  storefront in Nevada City, California)

- **6th and Detroit** (6thAndDetroit.com or
  the storefront in Long Beach, California)

- **Carter & Rose** (CarterAndRose.com or
  storefront in Portland, Oregon)

- **Black Springs Folk Art**
  (BlackSpringsFolkArt.com)

- ◆ **Fermata Woodworks** (FermataWoodworks.com)
- ◆ **Joyride Ceramics** (JoyrideCeramics.com)
- ◆ **Friend Assembly** (FriendAssembly.com)
- ◆ **VOL25** (VOL25.com)
- ◆ **Honeymoon Hotel** (HoneymoonHotel.Etsy.com)
- ◆ **Frida Clements** (FridaClements.com)

Where I Hunt for Vintage Finds:

- ◆ **Goodwill**
- ◆ **Etsy** (Etsy.com)
- ◆ **Craigslist** (Craigslist.org)
- ◆ **Ebay** (Ebay.com)
- ◆ **Flea markets**
- ◆ **Street fairs**
- ◆ **Yard sales**
- ◆ **Rummage sales**
- ◆ **Estate sales**
- ◆ **Everything but the House** (EBTH.com)
- ◆ **Homestead Seattle**

INSPIRING WOMEN

To find out more about the inspiring women featured in the book, check out these online sources:

Brandy Brown

WEBSITE: MarabouDesign.com

INSTAGRAM/PINTEREST/TWITTER /FACEBOOK: @maraboudesign

Photos on pages 18–24 of Brandy Brown's home

Diana La Counte

BLOG: OurCityLights.com

INSTAGRAM/PINTEREST/TWITTER /FACEBOOK: @ourcitylights

Photos on pages 42–48 of Diana La Counte's home

Brooke Eide

WEBSITES: Fonchie.com, FlintMade.co

INSTAGRAM: @brooke_eide, @_fonchie

PINTEREST: @brookebrooke

Photos on pages ii, 31 (upper left), 68–74, 114, 136, 142 (upper), 178 (top), 179 (top and bottom), 190, 196, and 198 of Brooke Eide's home

Kim Kogane

WEBSITE: FreshTangerine.com

INSTAGRAM/PINTEREST/FACEBOOK:
@freshtangerine

TWITTER: @freshtangerine_

Photos on pages 94–102 of Kim
  Kogane's space

Erin Perez Hagstrom

BLOG: CaliVintage.com

**INSTAGRAM/PINTEREST/TWITTER
/FACEBOOK:** @calivintage

Photos on pages 124–132, 139 (lower left),
  and 184 of Erin Perez Hagstrom's home

Laura Gummerman

BLOGS: TheBandWifeBlog.com,
ABeautifulMess.com

INSTAGRAM/PINTEREST:
@lauragummerman

Photos on pages 34, 139 (upper left and
  lower right), 142 (lower right), 156–164,
  179 (middle), 189, and back cover of Laura
  Gummerman's home

Moorea Seal

RETAIL WEBSITE: MooreaSeal.com

BLOG: Moorea-Seal.com

**INSTAGRAM/PINTEREST/TWITTER/
SNAPCHAT/FACEBOOK:** @mooreaseal

All other photos of Moorea Seal's space

Index

Note: Photographs are indicated by *italics*.

A

aloe plants, 144, *145*

animal fetishes, 141

animal skulls, *6*, 7, 108, *112*, 137–138, *139–140*, 141, 155

antiques, 22, 72, 75

antlers, 22, *23*, *109–110*, *140*, *146*, 147

art. *See* wall art and décor

art deco, 180, *181*

art nouveau, 181

authentic self, discovering your, 4, 6–8

author's personal story, 3–8, 29–33, 53–58, 79–84, 107–112, 137–141

B

Bauhaus design, 180, 182

Beautiful Mess, A, 157

bedroom, 105–133

Copper Pipe Necklace Display project, *120*, 121–122, *123*, 186

music playlist for sleep, 115

North Star Mirror project, 108, *116*, 117–119, 186

private sanctuary, creating a, *106*, 107–112, *109–110*, *112*

profile of Erin Perez Hagstrom, *124–132*, 125–133, 188

questions to consider about your own space, 113

Blakeney, Justina, 147

Blanket Ladder, Copper, DIY project for, *12*, 13, 185

blogs/blogging, 57, 58, 69, 111, 125, 157, 187–188

bohemian design, 3, 54, 58, 180, 183

Bracelet Display project, 122

Brown, Brandy, *18–24*, *19–25*, 187

C

cactuses, *55–56*, 144, *145*, 158, *158*, 160, *164*

CaliVintage, 125

candles, 53, 60

chairs, vintage styles of, 181–183

childhood, 4, 6–7, 8, 49

children, creating environment for, *127*, 128, 129, *130–131*

Citizenry, The, 4

clothes, scenting with lavender, 147

clothes and style, 11, 108, 111–112

color, 7, 108, 151

art and, 25, 154

associations, 174–175

buying vintage and, 133

joy and humor, design tips for, 49

psychology, 176–177

theory, 168–173

community, 21–22, 54, 57–58, 71

confidence, 7, 81, 96, 111–112

cookbooks, displaying, 37

Copper Blanket Ladder project, *12*, 13, 185

copper kitchen items, *31*, 33

Copper Pipe Necklace Display project, *120*, 121–122, *123*, 186

craft projects. *See* DIY projects

Craigslist, 69, 75

crystals, 147

D

design eras, vintage, 180–183

designers. *See* women, profiles of

design styles, types of, 178–179

Desk Hack project, Ikea, *88*, 89–90, 185

Diffuser, Essential Oil, DIY project for, *14*, 15–16, *17*, 185

dining room, 51–75

    celebrating friendship and family, *52*, 53–58, *55–56*

    Gold-Patterned Glassware project, *62*, 63, 185

    Macramé Wall Hanging project, *64*, 65–66, *67*, 185

    profile of Brooke Eide, *68–74*, 69–75, 187

    questions to consider about your own space, 59

    tips for hosting a dinner party, 60–61

DIY projects, 185–186

    Copper Blanket Ladder, *12*, 13, 185

    Copper Pipe Necklace Display, *120*, 121–122, *123*, 186

    Essential Oil Diffuser, *14*, 15–16, *17*, 185

    Floral Ice Cubes, *40*, 41, 185

    Gold-Patterned Glassware, *62*, 63, 185

    Herb Drying Rack, 30, 38–39, *39*, 185

    Ikea Desk Hack, *88*, 89–90, 185

    Macramé Wall Hanging, *64*, 65–66, *67*, 185

    Marbled Leather Mouse Pad, *91–92*, 93, 186

    Moon Phase Wall Hanging, 148–151, *149–150*, 186

    Nature Gallery Wall, *152*, 153–155, 186

    North Star Mirror, 108, *116*, 117–119, 186

Dlugolecki, Maja, 79

dreams and goals, 79, 81–84

dressing. *See* clothes and style

E

Eide, Brooke, *68–74*, 69–75, 187

elegance and whimsy, design tips for, 25

Elliott, Devyn, 32

Essential Oil Diffuser project, *14*, 15–16, *17*, 185

essential oils, combinations of, 16

F

family, 3–8, 21–22, 53–58, 70–72, 82, 84, 126–129, 138, 141

fear, 32–33

Flint, 70

Floral Ice Cubes project, *40*, 41, 185

flowers, 22, *23–24*, 37

folk style, 178

Fonchie Design, 70–71

frames, picture, 49, 154

Fresh Tangerine, 97–98

friends, 3–4, 6, 21–22, 53–58, 60–61, 71, 72, 111

furniture. *See* vintage

G

Gallery Wall, Nature, DIY project for, *152*, 153–155, 186

gender elements, balance of, 7, 108

gender roles, 29, 30, 108

glassware, for dinner party, 37, 60

Glassware, Gold-Patterned, DIY project for, *62*, 63, 185

gold accents, 20–21, 25

Gold-Patterned Glassware project, *62*, 63, 185

growth, personal, 29–33

growth, professional, 79–84

Gummerman, Laura, *156–164*, 157–165, 188

H

Hagstrom, Erin Perez, *124–132*, 125–133, 188

Hall, Kelli, 20

health and wellness, 30, 32, 43–47, 107–108, 141

    See also self-care

Hello Kitty, 44, *44*, 45, 47
Herb Drying Rack project, 30, 38–39, *39*, 185
humor and joy, design tips for, 49

I

Ice Cubes, Floral, DIY project for, *40*, 41, 185
identity and self-expression, 3–8, 82–84, 107–108, 111–112
Ikea Desk Hack project, *88*, 89–90, 185
Ikea furniture, repurposing, 98
imperfection, beauty in, 7, 71, 72, 79
inspiration, 30, 32, 37, 79–87, 98, 138, 141

J

jars, clear, *36*, 37
joy and humor, design tips for, 49

K

kitchen, 27–49
    finding peace in process, *28*, 29–33, *31*
    Floral Ice Cubes project, *40*, 41, 185
    Herb Drying Rack project, 30, 38–39, *39*, 185
    inspiring self-investment, tips for, 37
    profile of Diana La Counte, *42–48*, 43–49, 187
    questions to consider about your own space, 35
Kogane, Kim, *94–102*, 95–103, 188
Koger, Susan, 125

L

La Counte, Diana, *42–48*, 43–49, 187
Ladder, Copper, DIY project for, *12*, 13, 185
lavender, scenting clothes with, 147
leadership, tips for, 103
leaf place cards, 60
Leather Mouse Pad project, *91–92*, 93, 186

living room, 1–25
    Copper Blanket Ladder project, *12*, 13, 185
    defining your space and yourself, *2*, 3–8, *5–6*, *8*
    escaping technology, tips for, 11
    Essential Oil Diffuser project, *14*, 15–16, *17*, 185
    profile of Brandy Brown, *18–24*, 19–25, 187
    questions to consider about your own space, 9

M

MacPherson Leather Company, 93
Macramé Wall Hanging project, *64*, 65–66, *67*, 185
Marbled Leather Mouse Pad project, *91–92*, 93, 186
midcentury modern design, 30, 57, 71, 72, 97, 128–129, *129*, *132*, 159, 179, 180, 182
Mirror, North Star, DIY project for, 108, *116*, 117–119, 186
ModCloth, 125
mod design, 183
Montessori method, 128
Moon Phase Wall Hanging, 148–151, *149–150*, 186
MooreaSeal.com, *78*, 79–84, *80*, *83*, 186, 188
motivational quotes, 87
Mouse Pad, Marbled Leather, DIY project for, *91–92*, 93, 186
music playlist for sleep, 115

N

Native American heritage, 138, 141
nature, 22, 60, 135–165
    bringing the outside in, *136*, 137–141, *139–140*
    easy-care, indoor plants, 144–145, *145*
    Moon Phase Wall Hanging project, 148–151, *149–150*, 186

Nature Gallery Wall project, *152*,
153–155, 186

nonplant design ideas, 147

profile of Laura Gummerman, *156–164*,
157–165, 188

questions to consider about your own
space, 143

See also flowers; plants

necklace display, branch as, 147

Necklace Display, Copper Pipe, DIY
project for, *120*, 121–122, *123*, 186

North Star Mirror project, 108, *116*,
117–119, 186

O

office, 77–103

Ikea Desk Hack project, *88*, 89–90, 185

leadership, tips for, 103

Marbled Leather Mouse Pad project,
91–92, 93, 186

motivational quotes, 87

nurturing professional growth, *78*, 79–84,
80, *83*

profile of Kim Kogane, *94–102*,
95–103, 187

questions to consider about your own
space, 85

outdoors. *See* nature; plants

P

palms, ponytail, 145, *145*

parties and gatherings, 21–22, 37, 53–54, 72

Floral Ice Cubes project, *40*, 41, 185

Gold-Patterned Glassware, *62*, 63, 185

tips for hosting, 60–61

personality. *See* identity and self-expression

philodendrons, 144, *145*

pinecones, 147

Pinterest, 82–83

place cards, 60

plants, 71, *136*, 137, 138, *139*, 141, *142*, 143

easy-care, indoor types, 144–145, *145*

fake, 84, 137, 143, 147

Herb Drying Rack project, 30, 38–39,
39, 185

tips for decorating with, 165

See also nature

playfulness and joy, design tips for, 49

playlist for sleep, 115

process, finding peace in, *28*, 29–33, *31*

projects. *See* DIY projects

Q

quotes, motivational, 87

R

rain song, 141

resources, 185–188

retro design, 7, 158, 159, 179, 180

Rose, Jessica, 108

Royal Tenenbaums gallery wall, 45, *46*, *48*

rugs, kitchen, 37

rustic design, 178

S

Seal, Moorea, ix–xi, 186, 188

blog, 57, 58, 111, 188

MooreaSeal.com and, 79–84

personal stories of, 3–8, 29–33, 53–58,
79–84, 107–112, 137–141

seasons, 21–22, 53, 157–158, 160

self-care, 30, 32, 47, 107–108, 111–112,
113, 141

self-confidence, 7, 81, 96, 111–112

self-expression and identity, 3–8, 82–84,
107–108, 111–112

self-investment, ix–x, 37, 111–112, 128–129,
141, 143

skulls. *See* animal skulls

sleep, music playlist for, 115

snake plants, 145, *145*

sophistication, design tips for, 25

Southwestern design, 179

"spirit sisters," 57

style, personal. *See* clothes and style

styles, types of, 178–179

styles, vintage, 180–183

T

technology, tips for escaping, 11

thrifting, 75, 187

Trescott, Mickey, 32

U

utilitarian, 182

V

Venatory, The, 69

vintage, 75, 133, 180–183, 187

W

wall art and décor, 7–8, 79, 147

    color and, 25, 154

    Copper Blanket Ladder project,
      12, 13, 185

    frames, choosing, 49, 154

    Macramé Wall Hanging project, *64*,
      65–66, *67*, 185

    Moon Phase Wall Hanging project,
      148–151, *149–150*, 186

    Nature Gallery Wall project, *152*,
      153–155, 186

    North Star Mirror project, 108, *116*,
      117–119, 186

    See also specific room

wallpaper, plant-patterned, 147, 165

well-being, 107–108, 129, 137

wellness. *See* health and wellness

West Elm, 71, 84

whimsy and elegance, design tips for, 25

women, leadership tips for, 103

women, profiles of

    Brandy Brown, *18–24*, 19–25, 187

    Brooke Eide, *68–74*, 69–75, 187

    Diana La Counte, *42–48*, 43–49, 187

    Erin Perez Hagstrom, *124–132*,
      125–133, 188

    Kim Kogane, *94–102*, 95–103, 187

    Laura Gummerman, *156–164*,
      157–165, 188

women-powered businesses, 4, 79–84

Z

Zuni fetishes, 141

About the Author

MOOREA SEAL is a Seattle-based retailer, designer, author, and online curator who is known for her large following on Pinterest and mental health advocacy. With a desire to empower women and girls of all ages, she promotes a lifestyle of "Doing Good while Doing Great." Through her fashion and lifestyle brand, also named Moorea Seal, she gives back 7 percent of all proceeds to nonprofits. She is also the best-selling author of the 52 Lists series of journals.

Shop her store and learn more at MooreaSeal.com.

Notes

Printed in China

Published by Sasquatch Books

21 20 19 18 17   9 8 7 6 5 4 3 2 1

Editor: Hannah Elnan
Production editor: Emma Reh
Illustrations and lettering: Julia Manchik
Photographs: Marissa Maharaj
Design: Anna Goldstein
Copyeditor: Kristin Vorce Duran

Library of Congress Cataloging-in-Publication Data is available.

ISBN: 978-1-63217-035-4

Sasquatch Books
1904 Third Avenue, Suite 710 | Seattle, WA 98101
(206) 467-4300 | custserv@sasquatchbooks.com
www.sasquatchbooks.com